Praise for *The Tin Ring*

'Zdenka Fantalová is an extraordinary witness ... ... outpouring that happened in Terezín (Theresienstadt) during WWII. She ... ... u-mentary, *The Music of Terezín*, which I direc ... ... tic creativity that took place there. But *The Tin* ... ... re-pressible spirit of those times.'
Simon Broughton, director and producer

'Zdenka's ordeal ended in Bergen-Belsen, as, almost, ... er, as did a piece of advice given to her father when he was arrested. "Just keep calm." She did. It is a story that astonishes all who hear it.'
Eileen Battersby, literary correspondent, *The Irish Times*

'What an incredible story of one woman's fight for survival against unimaginable horror. This is such a courageous book.'
Susan Thomas

In a personal letter to Zdenka, Prime Minister Boris Johnson said:
'I know you do this with no thought of praise or reward, but allow me to offer my own gratitude for so bravely keeping your story alive and educating people across the country about the atrocities of the Holocaust. Without survivors like you having the courage to tell their stories, we might never understand what you, and millions of others, experienced. Your strength of character and optimism are an example to us all.'
Points of Light Award, 2020

'It would be impossible not to be profoundly moved by the poignant and harrowing story of this now elderly woman. This truth serves as a repudiation of the visceral hatred and violence represented by Auschwitz, Treblinka, Bergen Belsen and all the other monstrous Nazi extermination centres. *The Tin Ring* takes us into Dante's Hell but here is someone who has survived and emerged to give the lie to Hitler's confident belief that he could act with impunity and never be held to account; someone who is able to speak for the countless mothers, sisters, wives, and lovers whose kith and kin were slaughtered; someone able to channel the suffering, pain, and their shocking loss into a defiant testimony. Zdenka's story reminds us how great is the power of true humanity; the greatness of the power of love; the triumph of life over the ideology and culture of death. Here is a love story to rebuke the evil hate story of the Shoah.'
David Alton, **Lord Alton of Liverpool**

'I found this book inside the Manchester war museum and I'm glad I did, it's a truthfully heartbreaking story that I'd not come across before. I encourage anyone/everyone to read this, in fact - I've lent this book out so many times I've now lost my copy!'
Sarah Marie

'Zdenka Fantlová and her story made a lasting impression. She survived six concentration camps, endured horrors the like of which most of us can't begin to comprehend, yet never lost the will to live or her optimism for a better future. During her time in the camps she kept a little tin ring, made for her by her boyfriend. She risked her life to keep this humble object that meant so much to her.'
Fiona Bruce, journalist and television presenter

'The story of *The Tin Ring* is a testimony to the human spirit, the will to live and, above all, Zdenka Fantlová's fight for survival. Zdenka protected this little tin ring and her life with astonishing determination. Never falling into destructive self-pity, her compassion for other people, her sense of humour and her ability to take remarkable risks are just part of Zdenka's indomitable spirit.'
Rapport Magazine, 2020

'Zdenka's writing made me feel so deeply connected. I don't think there are words to express how moving and incredible her story is so I would just like to say thank you for giving people like me a tiny taste of understanding as to what people went through. It has definitely changed me and given me deeper empathy. No matter how hard our situation seems we can always rise above it and that we are capable of far more than we can ever imagine. I have also learned how important it is to always show respect and consideration to people as we can never imagine what they have experienced in their lives. Thank you so much for giving me this experience and I definitely recommend this book.'
Carmen Dyer

'Truly amazing and inspirational. Zdenka really is so incredible. Thank you so much for publishing such an extraordinary life story.'
Peter Devonald, scriptwriter and producer

'The life and fate of Zdenka Fantlová is unbelievable and yet that is what happened. Such was the world in a time of the deepest spiritual darkness in human history… I am full of admiration for her human greatness and nobility.'
Milan Jungmann, *Prague Literary Review*

'I have just read *The Tin Ring* which moved me to tears several times. The appalling horrors of the holocaust must never be allowed to fade. Words are inadequate to express my thanks to her for writing a book which portrays her courage and fortitude in the face of the most appalling circumstances. A book that is written without bitterness or rancour. A life-enhancing book which has made me realise how fortunate we are and the few things that really matter.'
Berenice Roetheli, London

'A story unlike no other survival story from the inconceivable horrors of life in Nazi concentration camps. A story which needs to be heard and shared. Utterly incredible, utterly inspiring, completely life-changing.'
Becky Bye, Goodreads

'Zdenka received a standing ovation of several minutes and then, she moved to a table where, for over an hour, she signed her books and talked to the schoolchildren and their teachers and parents, who were queuing round the hall to buy a copy of *The Tin Ring*.'
Winchester Literary Society

'An unforgettable memoir which deserves to be read for its unique story and for its shared message about the unrelenting human spirit.'
Publisher's Weekly

'Zdenka Fantlova is a remarkable individual. She has somehow emerged from the horrors of both Auschwitz and Belsen with her spirit unquenched. *The Tin Ring* is a humbling and inspiring testament to that astonishing achievement.'
Jonathan Dimbleby

THE TIN RING
MY MEMOIR OF LOVE AND SURVIVAL
IN THE HOLOCAUST

Zdenka Fantlová

Published by McNidder & Grace
21 Bridge Street
Carmarthen SA31 3JS
Wales, UK

www.mcnidderandgrace.com

New edition paperback 2022
© Zdenka Fantlová
First published in the United Kingdom 2010
Original paperback published in 2012, reprinted 2013, 2014, 2016
Translation by Deryck Viney
Published in Czech as *Klid Je Síla, Rek' Tatínek*, Primus, 1996
Published in German as *In der Ruhe liegt die Kraft, sagte mein Vater*,
Weidle Verlag, 1997
Published in the USA as *My Lucky Star*, Herodias, 2001
Published in Italian as *6 campi. Sopravvissuta a Terezín, Auschwitz,
Kurzbach, Gross-Rosen, Mauthausen e Bergen-Belsen*, TRE60, 2018

A catalogue record for this book is available from the British Library.

ISBN   9780857162298
Ebook 9780857162304

Designed by JS Typesetting Ltd, Porthcawl
Cover designed by Tabitha Palmer

Printed and bound in the UK by Short Run Press Ltd, Exeter, UK

To an unknown member of the British Army,
who, through his humanity,
saved my life in Bergen-Belsen in April 1945

Recommendation

by Renos K Papadopoulos PhD
Professor and Director of the Centre for Trauma,
Asylum and Refugees, University of Essex, UK

This book is unique in many ways. Not only is it an auto-biographical narrative of exceptional quality and sensitivity, not only does it relate events and experiences of an extraordinary life full of suffering, passion and resilience, not only does the author emerge as a most remarkable human being brimming with compassion, curiosity and zest for life but, above all, this book, in a most subtle way, is also highly original in its approach and this deserves to be acknowledged, appreciated, welcomed and applauded.

During a discussion, following the staging of an one-woman theatrical piece based on *The Tin Ring*, an eminent representative of a humanitarian organisation had the courage to voice a concern, characterising this book as 'dangerous'. The essence of his concern was that the main emphasis of the book is on hope and love and, therefore, there is a danger that its readers underestimate both the inhumanity and horrors of the events narrated as well as the devastating and damaging effects these have on their victims. This concern is understandable and valid. Testimonies of unspeakable brutalities, such as those committed by Hitler's Nazis, should convey in no ambiguous terms the clear message that these heinous acts should not be forgotten, that there should be no impunity for their perpetrators and that their destructive outcomes should always be remembered so that we endeavour to prevent their repetition.

However, what is of great importance is the manner in which the destructive effects on the victims is conveyed and the specific type of emphasis given. Usually, such accounts are based on an assumption of a seemingly logical equation that relates directly and causally the degree of brutality of the acts, to the degree of the damage inflicted on the victims: the more callous the events, the more serious the injuries (physical and psychological) suffered by the victims. Consequently, in order to condemn the viciousness of the perpetrators we tend to show how badly the victims have been scarred. Invariably, psychological dimensions of the traumatisation of the victims are advanced to underscore the gravity of the perpetrators' destructiveness.

Zdenka Fantlová writes with simplicity and directness, she conveys the pain and suffering she has endured in its raw nature, without sentimentality or exaggeration and yet, at the same time, she emerges not as a victim to be pitied, not as a broken person who has been reduced to an invalid as a result of her endless ordeals but as a person with intact human dignity and, if anything, even becoming stronger having survived these unthinkable horrors. Through the pages of this book, the reader witnesses unmistakably that the author, incredulous as it may be, succeeds in retaining a unique and admirable ability to reflect on her life and tribulations even while in the midst of the most unbearable losses, deprivation and humiliation. At no time does the reader sense that Zdenka abandons herself to becoming a mere victim of the cruel circumstances that her life brought her, to reacting impulsively to her immeasurable pain and anger; instead, she succeeds in preserving an inconceivable love for life and an unshakable belief in her own survival. She even writes explicitly that, whilst experiencing all the victimisation, she felt that she had a choice between accepting the identity of a victim and not accepting it.

This is truly astonishing and it is this that constitutes the main unique feature of this book. Books of this genre tend to emphasise either the severity of the damage inflicted on the victims or the heroism and resilience of the survivors. The complexity of this book consists in the inclusion of both whilst, at the same time, the clear message that emerges (and not trumpeted about in the book) is about the strength of the human spirit that can endure and survive even the most adverse possible conditions.

Such emphasis can, indeed, appear as 'dangerous' to all those whose job is to mobilise support for victims. To put it crudely, people are not likely to give money to support persons who survived adversity and are now faring well. People tend to support appeals that depict broken victims in desperate need for assistance. Images of starving children, severely injured persons, mourning mothers of killed children, destroyed homes and neighbourhood, miserable conditions of makeshift temporary shelters, all these touch people's hearts and make them donate to humanitarian causes.

Thus, this book, whilst being a personal narrative of an amazingly rich and excruciatingly painful life, it problematizes us and urges us to consider the complexity of such events and experiences. Without minimising the horrors, it is not dominated by them, without diminishing the enormity of the pain, it is not driven by it.

Another unique feature of this book, that needs to be highlighted, is the fact that it is written many years after the time of the events recounted. Given that it is now nearing seventy years since the end of the World War II, it is very likely that this may be the last book written by an actual survivor. However, what is more important to discern is that the great majority of the holocaust books are written by survivors who use their testimonies to create a space for them to reflect on what happened to them and to construct their new identity as survivors, in other words, their own writing is used almost for their own therapeutic purposes.

There is nothing wrong with this. However, this is not the case with Zdenka Fantlová. Because of her remarkable stance throughout her ordeal as well as the years that have passed since the events had occurred, this book is not a draft attempt used to formulate her ideas and emotions but the ripe product of a mature reflection that has been forged over the years of self-examination. In this sense, this book is also unique.

Above all, this book is an extremely rare testimony of defiance against brutalisation and humiliation, it is a humble expression of the power of endurance and love, it is written with sincerity and sensitivity and it is a book that makes us think and question life and human relationships in surprisingly refreshing ways.

Foreword

A suitcase – a simple suitcase with a name and a number scrawled on it. Neil Molloy stared at it. It seemed to stand out from all the hundreds of others piled high in the Holocaust Museum in Auschwitz concentration camp. Maybe it was the smell of old leather, the dust, the enormity of the significance of this huge pile of suitcases that prompted him to take a photograph of it. Neil is a sculptor in the University town of Durham. On his return home, he looked at the photograph and decided to make a stone copy of that suitcase. When it was finished, he carved the name and the number – just as it was on the original – Zdenka Fantl – S716.

Henry Dyson, Keeper of Fine Arts at the University of Durham was told about the suitcase and went to see it in Neil's studio. The simplicity and the starkness of its message moved him greatly. Henry decided that this solitary stone suitcase should be the centrepiece of a Holocaust Memorial. So he commissioned Neil to add a bag of clothes, a book, a shoe, an abandoned umbrella, scattered at random on the grass in the garden of St Aidan's College. This simple, uncluttered memorial serves to remind the generations of students of what happened in the Holocaust and, we hope, it will inspire them to make sure that it never happens again.

Zdenka's suitcase has become an emblem – a symbol of strength of will and determination to survive against all odds. It is unique, and yet it is one of millions. All old now;

all bearing the name of the owner. One of thousands of suit-cases now stacked in Holocaust museums all over the world; an emotive reminder of genocide; the destruction of human beings – not only Jews, but homosexuals who had to wear a pink triangle; gypsies; disabled people; Jehovah's Witnesses – anyone deemed unfit to be a member of Hitler's master race.

A suitcase! Isn't it strange how a suitcase – a transient, frail receptacle, can become the guardian of memories? A veritable museum of historical treasures; a custodian of art and music. Without that suitcase, I would never have recorded her wonderful little book, *The Tin Ring*, for the blind. Without that suitcase, I would never have known its author, Zdenka Fantlová; I would not have written to her, met her, and come to love and admire her.

Without that suitcase, I would not have the privilege and honour of calling her my friend. How did it happen?

I first saw the stone suitcase when I stood in a group on the grass at St Aidan's College in Durham on Sunday, October 12th 2014. Representatives of the University, the faculty, the students, Christians, Muslims, Jews, clergy of all faiths, all watched in silence as the Jewish Prayer for the Dead was read. It was deeply moving. Yet one important person was missing. The owner of that suitcase, Zdenka Fantlová, the author of *The Tin Ring*.

On a flight to Switzerland, Zdenka had seriously injured her arm, which necessitated immediate surgery. She was not well enough to come to Durham for the Dedication Ceremony. Although I did not know her, I keenly felt her absence and decided to write to her and describe the event to her. A few weeks later, she telephoned me.

"Were you pleased with the stone replica of your suit-case?" I asked. "I haven't seen it!" she replied.

Horrified, I realised that no one had thought to send her a photograph of the memorial. I quickly printed copies and sent them by special delivery as I knew she was leaving for Prague that week. On her return, she contacted me again, we met and there began a deep and lasting friendship.

Now it is 2022 and Zdenka is celebrating her 100th birthday. The past few years have been overshadowed by the pandemic. Like so many elderly folk, she has lived without the frequent visits of friends and admirers. It has not been easy for her. In the pre-Covid years, I have watched her talk to young people, inviting them to her home, telling them her story and urging them to make sure they tell their friends and their children what happened to her, how she survived but was left alone in the world as none of her relatives had survived. She always urged her young readers to make sure the horrors of the Holocaust "would never happen again."

Zdenka Fantlová is indomitable – an inspiration to us all.

If ever you are going through a stressful time, please read and digest the words she often writes when autographing *The Tin Ring*.

"Life is wonderful with all its ups and downs. Every day is a gift."

Ann Rachlin MBE, March 2022

Preface

When I came back to my home town after fifty years' absence, three of my former schoolmates asked me the same question: "What on earth happened to you and your family after the Germans took you off to the concentration camp in January 1942? What was your day-to-day life like, and how is it that you are the only one of your family to have survived – in fact, the only one of all those they took from this town?"

This set me thinking. If people of my own generation, even my closest friends, knew nothing of the life we led between 1942 and 1945, what notion of it could the younger generation have?

Those of us who actually survived the German extermination camps are the sole eye-witnesses of that era. There are not many of us still alive. And when the last of us dies we will take all our experiences to the grave with us. No one will ever be able to read about them or judge what it was like for us or what we thought about our world. Each of us endured and survived it in different ways.

Our memories form part, though only a small part, of the whole historic truth. I decided to attempt a portrayal of those events in which I became enmeshed as a seventeen-year-old girl.

Contents

Introduction

Travelling with an invisible map

The train from Prague stopped at the station in a provincial town. Several people got out, hurried across the platform, melted through a subway into the surrounding streets and sped homewards.

Among them was an elderly woman in an autumn suit, hatless and carrying only a shoulder bag. She had no luggage. She made her way slowly through the booking hall like someone who is in no hurry. There was no one to meet her, but she had not expected anyone. Coming out she took in the autumn air before stopping short at the wide steps that led down to the street. She cast her eyes around uncertainly, as if she had arrived here for the first time. Perhaps she was even a little nervous about going any further.

At the bottom of the steps stood a young lad leaning on his bicycle. He watched her for a moment and decided that the woman had no idea where she was or where she wanted to go. With a mixture of curiosity and goodwill he asked:

"Are you looking for somebody?"

She reacted slowly, as if woken from a dream. "Yes, I am."

"Do you know where they live?" "I do," she answered quietly.

"And do you know the way? If not, I can take you there."

"Thank you. You're very kind but I can find my own way," she said with a smile. Seeing he was not wanted, the boy got on his bike and rode off. The woman walked down a few steps and stopped again.

Here on the left there used to be an institute for the blind, she thought, searching her memory like someone snatching at a dream-vision glimpsed in the ragged web of morning slumber. There had once been a lawn in front of the building, she recalled, with sandy paths and a wire fence all around. Next to the fence there always stood a blind man wearing the institute's uniform and playing a harmonica. A sad, slow, invariable tune. He must have liked it. He seemed to be playing for his own pleasure.

But the blind man had vanished long ago. So had the lawn with its paths, and the institute itself.

Finally she walked down the rest of the steps and made her way into town. She knew the route exactly, as if following an invisible map. At times she felt she was returning from an afterlife. Everything was so familiar to her, each street, each stone, as if she were an old dog sniffing its way. She might have been invisible herself, for all the notice people took of her. At every step the scene was exactly as in the old days – and yet quite different. She passed a cemetery where they sold candles and asters on All Souls' Day. An inscription over the entrance had reminded visitors that the world was not their home forever:

What you are now, so once were we.
What we are now, you too will be.

She walked through a narrow gate leading into what had once been the medieval walled town. Beyond the gate stood an inn. *Na Strelnici*: "Hunter's Inn", with its own theatre, where a travelling company played when it came to town.

She remembered how during the day the actors would take their posters around and sell tickets from house-to-house for the evening show. They were like visitors from another world. It was always a great event when the players were in town. The auditorium was filled with wooden benches, yet there was never an empty seat. Even children were allowed in, if accompanied by a grown-up. All the old popular plays were in the repertoire: *The Miller and His Child*, *Lucerna*, *The Fire-Raiser's Daughter*, *A Night in Karlštejn Castle*, and so forth.

As long as the curtain was down there was a continual bustle, but as soon as it rose and the lights went out a mysterious world of unpredictable events emerged, holding all spellbound. From the stage there drifted a smell of glue, make-up, old costumes, wigs and all the other theatrical aromas combined. In its centre stood a large brown prompter's box. This was hard to see around, and you could hear each sentence of the play from inside before the actors even opened their mouths. But this bothered nobody; the magic of the performance was undiminished.

It was only a stone's throw from the theatre to the main square, the very centre of the world. People strolled there on evenings, and on Sundays, past the church, town hall, stores, savings bank, the Bata shoe shop and the florist's shop, *U Holubu*, that smelled like a perfumery.

Next door to the florist's shop stood Mr Jirsák's drapery store, where one used to get snippets of material for pasting onto puppets and making dolls' clothes.

One reminiscence set off another in the old woman's mind, like a ball of thread unravelling.

At the Štadlers' corner shop Mrs Mansfeldová sold not only sweets but tickets for the *Lidobio*, "People's Cinema". Children could sneak in secretly, wearing Mother's hat, to see adults-only films like *The Bengal Lancers* and *Grand Hotel*, or a Charlie Chaplin film.

The woman stopped in front of a new self-service store. It was not there before. In her mind's eye she saw a different picture. Here was where Miss Kamenná, known as Kamenka, had a little shop that sold balls of embroidering wool and cheap oddments for handiwork. And hoops, with sticks to drive them. On the other side was Mr jakobe's shop that smelled of leather satchels and new school bags.

Next to him was Mr Flajšhans, with his textiles and haberdashery. He always stood in front of his shop, intoning in an old Czech dialect:

"Don't go down to the river, it's deep there, mighty deep!"

Directly opposite was the apothecary, "At the Sign of the White Stork". This shop smelled like a hospital. One came here to collect medicine whenever someone was ill. Behind the counter was a long row of china jars with labels in Latin. The chemist in his white coat would make up the prescribed mixture, weighing out the ingredients on tiny apothecary's scales. Next door was the grocery where one could buy, the notice proclaimed, both homemade and imported goods. The proprietor had a cage in his back yard where he kept fox cubs. Poor things, they must have gone crazy, locked up like that. He always tried to entice her in to "see his puppies". But she wouldn't be enticed. What she would have really liked was a bag of peanuts, but he never offered her those. So she only went to the grocer's when she had to, to buy extra fine ("thrice-ground") poppy seed for the kitchen.

Next door, Stancl the confectioner had the world's best sweetmeats. One often bought them for after Sunday dinner. And what "afters" they were! Chocolate cream puffs, rum cake, cream tart, whipped cream rolls, marzipan potatoes with chocolate filling and all kinds of things. Ice-cream was scooped up from a china pot with a big wooden spoon. What ice-cream it was!

On the corner was Mr Tajbl's drugstore. Two huge jars of jellies stood on the counter. One lot white, and one pink. Sometimes he would spare a few for the children.

Opposite him, in a narrow street alongside the town wall, had been a dark little shop where one had to walk up two stone steps and pull a bell string at the door. There, as a child, she used to buy her fortune in a magic envelope for one Czech crown, and quivered to see what the card would foretell. At the next corner was an inn and a pork butcher's shop, where, at five o'clock each afternoon, was sold the best meatloaf ever. It was brought to the counter on a silver tray, smoking and smelling heavenly. A portion wrapped in paper just had to be tried as soon as you were outside the shop.

There was an open market every Friday on the square. Farmers' wives came from all around to sell their butter, blueberries, mushrooms, geese, ducks, hens and pigeons. They spread their wares out on sacking over the cobblestones, a different row for each. A row of butter, another row of blueberries, and so on. The butter came in two-pound lumps, with a pattern cut on the top, all wrapped in huge green leaves. Blueberries were measured out from baskets by the litre with long-handled tin scoops and poured into the customer's pot.

Her mother used to have her own little knife for tasting the butter. She went up the line sticking it into each block, shutting her eyes and passing judgement.

"No, not this one. Let's try the next."

Only after trying several samples would she make her purchase. The old woman remembered that as a little girl she was dreadfully embarrassed and ashamed of her mother. She hated market days. Anca, the servant girl, had to come along to carry the shopping home in string bags.

The biggest excitement was the monthly fair on the square. There were dozens of stands set up, one selling bags of Turkish delight, another roasted almonds. There was always a stand with a parrot pulling horoscope cards out of a box so that people could buy them and see what fate had in store for them. Earthenware pots and pans for dolls' houses were laid out on sacking in another spot. Next to those was a stand full of coloured balloons. But the biggest draw of all was the wizened old blindfolded sorceress, Klamprdonka. She sat on a high chair in her bright skirt and black shawl, answering the questions her master put to her.

"Tell us, Klamprdonka, what has this gentleman got in the left pocket of his jacket?"

And she always knew. It was real magic and everybody clapped.

A few blocks further on there was a big empty space called *Na pátku*, where the Kludský circus would put up its marquee festooned with coloured electric bulbs. There were elephants, lions whining wearily in the cage, and a ringmaster calling the crowds in:

"Come and see what you have never seen before, ladies and gentlemen! Trained lions, an elephant dancing on bottles, acrobats performing miracles on the tightrope! Not for three crowns, not for two crowns, but for just one single crown! Come along, come along, you won't be disappointed!"

People poured in excitedly, scared stiff in case the acrobats fell off the high wire. There was a whiff of some alien world about the *Na pátku* ground. When the circus troupe left, the gypsies arrived. As a youngster, she had envied them their caravans and curtained windows, their life of wandering from place to place, and how the gypsy girls went around barefoot in long skirts with hair flying. That, she thought, was the real bohemian life.

If you went from the circus site along the old moat road you came to the great Sokol hall with its spacious sports ground. The gymnasium provided moral as well as physical exercise and even trained youngsters for the nationwide Sokol sports festivals at Strahov in Prague.

The Sokol hall was also the centre of the town's culture and entertainment, and the setting for great occasions. The famous actor, Vojta Merten, came from Prague to give the children a great theatrical treat, a play entitled *How Kašpárek* – the traditional Czech boy-hero – *Rescued the Princess from the Clutches of the Wicked Black Magician*. As a little girl she had been terrified when she saw Kašpárek starting to climb through a window into the Magician's chamber; she had sobbed aloud and run up to the stage to tell him not to go inside. Kašpárek interrupted the performance, came to the footlights, and reassured her that everything would turn out all right. When they got home afterwards her brother tattled on her and she was scolded for crying in public and holding up the show.

All kinds of social events took place in the Sokol hall. One day it would be an amateur theatrical performance. Another time, the great Jan Kubelík appeared as a guest artist, playing his violin. Sometimes they showed films, sometimes they held dancing classes or end-of-term balls. At Shrovetide there would be a masked ball and a firemen's ball. And then all the national celebrations.

On 7 March there was a school festival for President Masaryk's birthday. A male choir would sing "Glory to You, Our Nation's Greatest Son!" For Independence Day, 28 October, the hall was decorated with the national colours and flags, two palm trees were set up on each side, under the platform, and the national anthem rang out. Everyone felt proud of his country and determined to lay down his life for it. On the day itself there was a great parade with Sokol members and World War I legionaries forming a long procession that marched proudly in time to a brass band. Red-blue-and-white flags flew from every roof and window.

Crowds lined the pavements where they passed and shouted the Sokol greeting "Zdar!"

Those were the great occasions, the important days. The year was full of them. From the Great Hall of the Sokol building you could cross into the Little Hall where puppet performances were held for the children every Sunday at two o'clock. Wooden benches were set out for the spectators and a red curtain decorated with golden tassels hid the stage. When the bell had rung three times, the lights went out and the curtain rose. Everyone opened their eyes wide and held their breath.

Sometimes the curtain rose on a rustic room where Hloupý Honza – "Simple Simon" – was setting out to explore the world with a sack of sweet buns on his back. Sometimes it revealed a village green where people were discussing how best to help Simon kill the dragon. Or it might be a dark corner of the woods, with danger lurking everywhere. The finest sight of all, a royal chamber with majestic thrones in red and gold on which the king and queen were sitting, wearing their crowns. Every Sunday it was a different tale. Kašpárek releasing the princess from the spell. Kašpárek killing the wicked dragon, or finding the stolen treasure. Kašpárek and the robbers. Kašpárek and Kalupinka. Kašpárek was the greatest hero in the world. No one was ever like him.

The old woman walked on a little further until she found herself in front of a new residential block. But what she saw in her mind was very different. This had been the garden known as Prajzler's. Inside a wooden gate, there had been rows of vegetables growing – carrots, radishes, lettuce, kohlrabi, strawberries and everything imaginable. They were on sale in a little wooden shed on one side. In front of it was a huge water tub; Mrs Prajzlerová would pull out of the vegetable beds whatever was asked for, lettuce or radishes, and rinse them in the water. And one could take them home as fresh as fresh could be.

"Home"? Why, naturally. Home is forever. The firm ground beneath our feet; certainty and order, now and forever. The whole family together. There is no other way of life.

Or, is there?

She walked on through the streets, past homes and gardens which had long since vanished. What had replaced them were empty spaces, houses pulled down to make room for traffic and street-widening, a new circular road. The old stream that once flowed past, lined at Easter with catkin-covered pussy willows, had been filled in. New supermarkets, new notices, new people. Not a single familiar face. No one recognised her. At times she felt she had strayed into the wrong town. All that was left were the low hills on the horizon and the hazy blue woods around about. They alone had resisted time and progress. So she was right, after all. She reminded herself why she had come, and walked on to a point where three narrow streets used to meet.

On one corner used to be a fire station. On the opposite one, a tobacco booth. The third street led to the river. But everything had sunk into the abyss of time except for one building. "Our" home. Emerging suddenly from her memory was a large, turn-of-the-century three-storey house with a baroque balcony. All the neighbouring buildings on both sides had vanished. Now this one stood alone, like a silent witness of a different age, of long ago happenings. It seemed to have risen up from the very depths of her mind's well, long overlaid with layers of five different lives spent in other lands, other epochs, amongst other folk.

It struck her how much this home of hers had aged. It was like meeting a close school friend years later and finding that the youngster was now old and greyhaired. She could only wonder at the apparition, from which plaster had fallen to reveal bare bricks. The windows were grey and dusty, as if time had made them sightless. The front steps were all broken, and cobwebs filled the doorway. She stood silently before it as we stand by an overgrown grave that holds the remains of someone we have loved.

She felt she had arrived here from far away, from beyond the boundaries of space and time. No one ever came out of this house now, no one ever went in. She alone stood here. A living person watching a dead building. The longer she stood and gazed, the more confused she was by the gulf between what she remembered and what she saw in front of her. The house symbolised something from a life long gone. What had happened here seemed almost five centuries removed. Time itself seemed unreal. Had we merely fluttered like blown leaves, landing at random? Did we feel at home only when we had firm ground underfoot and a loved one by our side?

She felt like someone waking from a dream, confused about who or where she was and needing to wait a little for the scattered pieces to settle down again in their right places.

At the back of the space where she stood she noticed a little pile of planks. The builders had evidently left them there for tomorrow's work.

She sat down on them as, in years past, she might have settled on a tree trunk felled in the forest, and asked herself: "How did it all happen? Where were we, before we came here? Where did it all start?"

1

Grandfather

It really began with Grandfather, as the parish records of Cerhonice show.

Josef Mautner, originally of Blatná in southern Bohemia, makes his first appearance in Cerhonice in or after 1865 as proprietor of the taproom of the manorial brewery in the lord's house. Later he also leased the manorial inn at No. 10 Cerhonice. He was a corn dealer, too.

According to tradition, he was on close terms with the Cerhonice Administrator, Father Hugo Zahnschirm. Father Hugo was a monk of the Premonstratensian order from Schlägl monastery in Upper Austria, to which Cerhonice had belonged from 1688 until 1920. In Cerhonice, the Administrator, as the Abbot's deputy, represented the feudal authority.

Legend even has it that the pair of them, Mautner and the Administrator, used to sit conferring together on the two celebrated oval stones in front of the Cerhonice manor house.

Despite being a Jew, Mautner was not only the Administrator's advisor in commercial matters, but brokered all the affairs and appeals of the manorial staff and the common folk of Cerhonice. What Mautner said was accepted.

He evidently did well in the village. As early as 15 March 1868 Josef Mautner and his wife, Rosalie, bought from Jan Toman, a cottager, one part of his garden opposite the castle near the Pruhony road. In exchange for it he gave Jan Toman nine roods of good arable land in the Pod Pruhony area. This became known as Jew's Field.

On the plot he acquired Josef Mautner built a large brick house with several living rooms, a shop and a small reception hall. Next to it he put up a barn for six head of cattle and a number of sheds. A well was sunk in the courtyard.

The shop was approached from the village green by several sets of wide stone steps. As well as having a trading licence, Josef Mautner also obtained a licence to sell beer, so that from 1880 onwards there were virtually two inns in Cerhonice.

Mautner's taproom was in fact part of the family home, with doors leading onto the hallway, the shop, the reception room and a small annex at the northwest corner of the building. The shop sold all manner of daily necessities. The reception hall, quite a spacious one, hosted dance evenings – *musiky* – up until World War II.

In 1890 Josef Mautner lost his first wife; his second, Josefa, became joint owner of No. 50. She bore him one daughter, Barbora, or Betty, on 21 March 1897. Betty grew up to be a beautiful girl with dark eyes and braids rolled up into two little buns over the ears, as was the fashion then.

Old Mautner died around 1910.

They were a good, caring Jewish family. In the little corner room Josef's unmarried brother Jáchym had lain bed-ridden in pain for many years, paralysed by a stroke and tended by his sister-in-law.

The Mautners of Cerhonice came to a tragic end. From the beginning of World War I Josefa suffered fits of deep depression. During one bout, in the spring of 1916, she left the house early in the morning and ran to the Lomnice stream at Mirotice, more than three kilometres away, near the Karlov estate of the Schwarzenbergs. There she was found drowned in a deep pool.

So Betty was left entirely on her own. She was 18.

2

A fateful meeting

Arnošt Fantl was a fine young man with blonde hair and smiling blue eyes, who had just started an apprenticeship in brokering iron ore to steel factories and travelled around the area visiting customers.

One day, bound for Cerhonice on foot, he saw black clouds gathering in the sky. He was still in the fields when a great storm broke. Running through the rain, he could hardly see his way. At last he made it, soaked to the skin, into the first inn he could find in the village. Bursting through the door, he stood dumbfounded. For there behind the bar stood the lovely Betty, with her mass of brown hair, in a white blouse. Her black eyes rested on him for a moment. He stared back at this vision as if struck by lightning.

After he had had a meal and dried himself he knew he had to catch a train back home to Blatná. When the storm had passed, he persuaded Betty to accompany him to the station. She agreed, and as the train went off she stuck out her tongue at him. It was love at first sight and he knew that beautiful Betty was the only one for him.

He visited her whenever he had the time, and she fell deeply in love with him. Apart from being so fond of him, she was no longer on her own now and had someone she could entirely depend on.

In due course Arnošt helped Betty to sell the inn property, No. 50 Cerhonice, to one Anna Smolová of Malcice, with a few acres of land thrown in.

So ended the Mautner dynasty in Cerhonice. Betty moved to Blatná and very soon, in 1918, she married Arnošt. The wedding was at the Hotel Bristol in Prague. She looked wonderful in white, with a veil and a wreath on her head. The rabbi who conducted the wedding ceremony included these words of rare wisdom in his address:

"Happiness," he said, "is something you will only find at home. You would be looking for it in vain anywhere else."

But he hardly needed to tell them that. They were ardently in love and blissfully happy. They were my parents.

For their honeymoon they went to Vienna – the first time they had ever left the Cerhonice region. Vienna was all bustle, with its fine buildings, theatres, coaches, shop windows, music and culture. They were entranced.

When they returned they settled in Blatná, in the upstairs floor of a cottage near Blatná Castle. In September 1919, they had their first child, Jiríček. He was my brother. He was a weakly child and they feared for his life. They used to lay him in the tiled oven where it was warm and hold a mirror in front of his face to see that it misted over and showed he was still breathing. But Mrs Rázová, the midwife, helped to pull him through and he survived. I was born two-and-a-half years later, a lusty little girl (I was told) and highly inquisitive. My first great experience occurred when I was three.

There was a big event in Blatná. It was a Sunday, and new bells were being installed in the church steeple. The whole town turned out to watch. Father and Mother and Jiríček all went along, but I was left behind at home with Grandfather. There was going to be a big crowd, they said, and I was still too small. So off they went. My disappointment was so great I thought I would never get over it. Why had I been singled out to stay at home, when I was the one who was keenest of all to see the bells? And how was I going to see them if I had to sit at home with Grandfather keeping guard over me?

I decided I just had to see those bells. But there was little time to spare. The minutes were running out. Outside on the streets the whole population of Blatná was watching with excitement to see how they would pull those gigantic bells up into the tower. Suddenly I noticed that Grandfather had gone to sleep with his pipe in his mouth. My moment had arrived. I ran out of the room, down the stairs, into the hall and out through the front gate.

The part of the street in front of our house, with its good view of the church, was crammed with people. Though I was only knee-high, I wriggled my way between them like I was going through a dense forest, until I found Mother. How I knew it was her I cannot say, but it was. I pulled at her skirt until she bent down to see who was bothering her. When she saw me she was scared at first, but then she smiled and nudged Father, to show him what a brave little girl he had. With a jolly laugh he held me up high above the heads of the crowd and then sat me on his shoulders to have a good view. And what did I see?

I saw the bells, already hauled up to the right height, just as they were falling neatly into their places in the tower. So I hadn't missed it. I was beside myself with excitement and felt I had won the biggest victory of my three-year-old life. In the end even Grandfather forgave me for having given him the slip.

I was stealing things while playing in the street, I was told, though I didn't think of it that way at the time. Mrs Boušová ran a small grocery store next to our house. There were two stone steps leading up to it. Two sacks, rolled down to halfway, always stood on the pavement on each side of the door. One was full of prunes and the other of peanuts. When I was playing in the street I used to circle around those sacks like a kitten around a saucer of cream. It wasn't the prunes that interested me, but the peanuts. I could have asked Mrs Boušová if I could have a few – but then, she might have said no. So I set about getting them without asking questions.

I ran indoors and put on a pinafore like a good little girl, then ran straight back to the sacks. There I filled up my pinafore with a supply of peanuts and then hurried off to the back garden to eat them. But there was a snag. At the bottom of the garden was a dark shed with a huge ace of spades poster stuck on the wall. It depicted a creature with long claws, bare fangs and great yellow eyes. I was scared stiff because it looked at me and knew all about me.

From that day on I never went into the shed, nor around to the grocer's again.

My father often took me for a walk to Blatná Castle. We had to cross a wooden drawbridge under which there were water lilies growing with leaves like lettuces. After that followed a long, long walk through the wonderful Castle grounds. Those were idyllic days for a child, carefree and full of affection.

And then came a great change.

3

Moving to another town

Early in 1925 Father decided we should move to Rokycany, a larger town with iron foundries, a rolling mill and steel furnaces, where he could make a much better living. He was an able and hardworking man, much loved for his good humour. He longed to provide his beloved Betty and their two children with a good life, free from worry, and a better education than he had enjoyed himself. In this new town there were two elementary schools, a secondary council school and a grammar school.

So a new stage in our life began.

The house we moved into welcomed us with open arms. It almost smiled upon us. Father installed his parents, who were getting on in years now, on the second floor. We had our flat on the first. There was a pretty balcony over the street, and a covered gallery over the courtyard behind. It had several rooms, plus a big kitchen, with another little bedroom behind that. It seemed as big as a castle and the hall was so long I could ride my tricycle along it.

On the street side of the ground floor my father had his iron brokerage, with an office and storerooms behind it. Grandfather immediately planted himself, with his pipe, in the corner behind the counter. He occupied this seat from first thing in the morning, and though there was an assistant to serve customers, he kidded himself that he was busy all day long. He only left the shop at midday to join us in the kitchen, sit down at the table, bang his fist on the table and shout:

"Let's see some food served!"

Father's business was soon established and our new life got off to a promising start. Peace, love and happiness reigned in the family and it never occurred to anyone that things could be otherwise. Father spent all week travelling and seeing customers, but he could never wait for Friday to come around so that he could go back to his beloved Betty and his children. In fact, he had found at home exactly the domestic bliss that the rabbi had talked about at their wedding. There seemed no reason to believe that this family idyll wouldn't last forever.

But it was not to be.

We were struck an unexpected blow. Mother fell victim to a mysterious and unexplained malady. She started getting high temperatures and no one could identify the cause. Dr Drábek, who had visited us children whenever we were ill – I remember how cold his ear felt when I had a fever and he laid it on my chest – thought she had blood poisoning.

My brother and I went to stay with neighbours so as not to be in the way. Father used to come around to see us, his eyes red from crying. I scribbled a note for him to take to Mother, saying we would go for a walk together as soon as she was well, and I would take my new little red umbrella.

"Yes, of course I'll give her your little letter," my father promised, and wiped away his tears.

Then things happened very quickly.

Two days later Father arrived to pick us up. Mother wanted to see us. We walked along, with Father holding us by the hand, me on his right side and Jiríček on his left. As we walked into her bedroom she was lying on a pile of white pillows with her lovely brown hair spread all over them. As soon as she saw us she buried her face and started sobbing bitterly. The pain of seeing her darling children for what might be the last time was too much for her to bear.

Early the following morning she died. It was a sunny day, 5 November 1925.

She was just twenty-eight.

Jiríček was six years old, and I was three-and-a-half.

The whole town escorted Mother to her grave. She was universally loved, and had always shown understanding for other people. The death of his beloved Betynka was more than my father could bear. He could not imagine life without her, and her last words were forever ringing in his ears:

"Arnošt, my beloved, thank you for the lovely seven years we have had together."

It was now that he conceived a desperate plan. Without her, his life had lost all meaning. So he would end it. He would kill himself and take his children with him to the next world, where we would all meet again.

He found a revolver. A few days after the funeral he made up his mind to use it.

He waited until we were fast asleep, telling himself it would be easier then. He would not have to look into our eyes, and so he could do what he had to do quickly and properly. First me, then Jiríček, then himself. Just like that.

His decision made, he came up to my cot and pointed the revolver at me. At that moment I woke up. As soon as I saw him standing over me I gave him a big smile. He glanced at me and the revolver fell from his hand. Mother must have been watching from heaven and made it happen like that. Certainly she would have wanted us all to carry on, even without her. Father seemed to hear her voice; he threw the revolver away and found the strength in himself to live on.

In later years he was to tell me how important it was to have a companion in life. "A shared pleasure is a double pleasure; a shared pain is half a pain."

"If you ever suffer a deep grief, immerse yourself in work. That's the only thing that can save you."

Which is what he did. He threw himself into his business, working not only for himself but for the other ironworks in the area, and he cooperated with them very well.

We hardly saw anything of him. We were looked after by his old parents who still lived in the house. But that was a temporary arrangement. He realised, though he was loath to admit it, that his parents were entitled to a quieter old age than looking after us all day. So another mother was needed. As far as he was concerned, he could not imagine having a second wife. But his parents evidently agreed with his second thoughts and so, reluctantly, he began to look around. Several matchmakers were consulted.

Young widower with two children seeks ...

An unmarried clerical worker from a large, respectable Jewish family in Pardubice was found. Named Ella, both her parents were alive, as well as two brothers and two sisters. The sisters, Irma and Marta, were married, and so was her oldest brother, Robert. Only the youngest of the family, Karel, was still single, and was therefore called Little Charlie – Karlícek. Ella had never had many offers, it seemed, and was getting on a little for marriage. She decided to accept my father, and indeed she was fond of him. But it always remained a one-sided love.

One day Grandmother announced to us that a new mother was going to move in, and took us accordingly to the local barber. He was told to cut my hair so that it covered only half my ears, and to give me a fringe. I looked as if I had a pudding-basin on my head, but that didn't worry me.

The day arrived for the new mother to introduce

herself to us. She brought her own mother with her, our new grandmother-to-be. The two of them stood next to a window in a separate room, waiting for us to be brought in for the official audience. I was first. There I stood in front of this strange lady who was wearing a dark blue woollen dress with a row of large white mother-of-pearl buttons running down the centre. I was so impressed with those lovely shining buttons I couldn't take my eyes off them. Nothing else about the meeting interested me.

The wedding took place on 3 June 1926, at the Na Veselce hotel in Pardubice. The couple went for their honeymoon to Smokovec in the Tatra mountains. Our new mother looked happy enough. For my father, the pleasure came from enjoying the mountain scenery and forest air.

I never had the feeling that I had a new loving mother; it was more like having a governess who was in charge, running the household and making sure we always had enough to eat and wore the right clothes.

So I really grew up on my own. We had a cook, Katty, and a chambermaid, Anca. I used to sit with them on a stool in the kitchen; that was where I really felt at home. They were fond of me and I shared all my secrets with them. One time I saved Katty's life when she choked on a piece of bread. I kept thumping her back until the lump shifted, though I'd never been taught any first aid. Katty came from a German area in the Sudetenland and didn't know much Czech. When she caught her first breath she gasped: "*Stenycko neny telala bum bum tak Kattyno pytech!*" Zdenka no go bang-bang, Katty a goner!

The following year Father sent us for a summer holiday in Pec, near Domazlice, and Anca came too. I loved that. There was an area behind the hotel with little chairs and tables, so we could have breakfast out in the sun instead of in the kitchen like we did at home. Beyond that was an enclosure with a fishpond and grass around it. There were geese there but you could sit and pick the dandelions. The pond was muddy. I had rubber bathing shoes so I didn't mind much, even if it was rather squelchy. Jirka and I – he wasn't Jiríček, Little Jírka, any more – used to go off on our own into the surrounding forest to collect blueberries in a painted jug.

We also waded through a cold stream that was so clear you could see the bottom. When the sun shone on it the water glittered like silver. There were forget-me-nots on the bank, where we would sit on the grass watching the shiny trout dart upstream.

There was a chicken yard by the hotel too, with hens and a cock. Around it was a wooden fence with a little latch gate. This place was strictly out of bounds on account of the cock-bird, who was supposed to be wild and dangerous. But I was never one to miss anything, so I determined to have a look at him. One day when nobody was around I secretly opened the gate and went inside. There he was, looking proudly around as if he were monarch of the world, while his hens quietly pecked and cackled. I started running after him. At first he circled away from me but then suddenly got angry, turned around, flew in my face and grabbed my neck in his claws. I shouted at the top of my voice. Several people rushed from the hotel. Seeing what was up, they caught the bird and dragged it off me. The hotel owner was quite beside himself, fearing it might have pecked my eyes out.

This all happened when I was five. The year after that there was another big change in the family scene.

4

A new little sister

We had a telephone in the office. In homes such things were still rarities, but for businesses they were indispensable. Our phone was a big black instrument attached to the wall. First you had to take the receiver down off the hook. Then you turned a handle on the side and the exchange answered. Our telephone number was 5.

One day Father called me into the office to talk to somebody on the phone. It was Mother calling from Prague to tell me I had a new baby sister. I felt rather as if I had been given a new toy. I couldn't wait for her to be brought home so that I could put her in her carriage and take her for a ride in the town square where everyone could see her. After that I would play with her in the house.

Father took us to Dr Boruvka's nursing home in Prague. Mother was in bed and next to her, in a cradle all cushioned and curtained, lay a little creature with black hair and the tiniest hands and fingers I had ever seen. They had decided to call her Lydia.

When Mother arrived home with the baby, everything turned out differently. My dreams of pushing my little sister in a carriage were dashed. A private nurse was hired. She was a German called Sister Gaube. She wore a light brown nurse's uniform and a matching veil with a white headband.

The little baby was entirely hidden from view in her white wicker cradle, behind a white frilled curtain.

Sister Gaube was very strict and wouldn't let me go near the cradle. I couldn't understand why, and felt shut out of everything. They managed to kill in the bud all my love for the new child, all my interest in her. So I dug my heels in. I stopped asking to see her, showed no further interest and turned my back on her.

However, I was rescued from this crushing childhood disappointment by the next stage in my life, the most important of all.

5

School

On 1 September 1928 Grandfather took me to school for the first time. The school was in one of the parish houses, standing on a small estate just behind the church. Our grade, IA, was on the first floor, up a wooden staircase worn thin over the years. We were greeted by the teacher assigned to the class, Anna Sedlácková. This woman was to become the most important influence in my life. I respected and acknowledged her as on a par with my father, and she guided us carefully and conscientiously from the first grade right up to the fifth.

If school is the foundation of life, Anna Sedlácková certainly laid it for me. She taught us not only reading, writing and arithmetic, but affection for the Czech language and for poetry. I sat in the front row, taking in every word she said. I loved school and I loved her.

She lived close to us and passed our home on the way to school. From half past seven I would be waiting for her to carry her bag of books. She was tall and slim, of an age I could only guess at. More on the older side than the young, I judged. She combed her dark hair straight back and tied it in a knot behind. She was always kind and helpful and took her role as teacher and mentor seriously. I learned quickly and always did my homework properly, mainly to please Anna Sedlácková.

Our school had a special charm in the wintertime. It was still dark when you set off from home, but there were already lights in the windows to welcome you and the stove had been lit to make the classrooms pleasantly warm.

In fact, I felt happier at school than at home. My bench neighbour was Vera, and the two of us became best friends. She was an only child and I felt like one – Jirka had his own chums – so we took to one another like sisters.

Vera lived just the other side of our courtyard. I only had to run along a path and I was already in her cottage. Her father was a men's and boys' outfitter and a keen Sokol gymnast. He marched in processions wearing the Sokol uniform, a cape tied with a cord, high boots, and Sokol cap with a feather in it. Vera's mother baked the most marvellous griddle cakes on a greased hotplate, dusted with cinnamon. Her father used to run around from the workshop with his measuring tape hanging around his neck and down five of them at a go. Her mother also used me as an example for her own daughter:

"Look how nicely Zdenka does her hair, Verunka. And you go around looking like a scarecrow!" I was made more than welcome in their home. Whatever Vera did, I did too. If she wore a white dress and carried a little basket of roses on Corpus Christi at Easter, her mother would find me a white dress and basket of petals too, so that I wouldn't feel out of things and could join the procession with Vera. I wasn't scared of my own mother seeing me on this Christian holiday, because she never went to that kind of event.

I felt very important, walking alongside Vera and scattering petals in a circle around me along the path to Calvary, where we stopped at every turning in front of the figures of the Holy Family. After the procession was over I went back to Vera's to change and then off home quite innocently, as though nothing happened.

We both joined the Sokols and were keen on sports. We used to go to the Áleje sports centre together, where there was a track-and-field sports ground and a weed-overgrown tennis court. We got hold of a couple of rackets, each with at least three broken strings, and some worn out tennis balls. To hold the balls we crocheted little red nets from pieces of wool. We played for all we were worth, shouting the scores in English (even though we didn't understand the words) and pretending to be world champions.

Close by the Áleje was a swimming pool. There were several wooden changing cabins with the knots in the walls poked out, and a small hole called the Great Pool, fed from the dam by a little stream. First we blew up our yellow water wings, put them on and lowered ourselves down the slippery wooden steps into the stream.

The bottom was muddy and the banks were overgrown with willow trees and willow herb. There we jumped along on one leg, pushing the water to each side with our arms, and so learned a kind of breast stroke. Only after that did we have the courage to go into the Great Pool, feeling we had passed a great test of maturity. The only annoying thing were the swimsuits, which in those days were always woollen, never dried properly, and felt horribly itchy.

In the winter we explored the low hills nearby on heavy wooden skis and imagined we were in the Alps. Sometimes we careered down the slopes on these skis, sometimes on sleds.

What we enjoyed most of all was skating on the fishpond. Our skates were of the kind that fitted over the shoes and were tightened with a key, which you had to keep in your pocket. First we cast our discerning eyes over the ice to see if it were thick enough to support us. Then we sat down on a log, put on our skates, which had spiral points like violin scrolls, and tightened them with the key. Now we were ready to go. We learned to make forward and backward turns, and even to jump from one foot to the other like Sonya Henie in the cinema newsreels.

Winter was lovely, and summer too. And so were spring

and autumn. Our life was spent in the open air, in the forests and meadows around about, along the rivers and ponds. We were more out of doors than in.

But then elementary school finished and grammar school began. Before the end of term, Father bought me a leather-bound scrapbook and wrote one of his pieces of wisdom in it:

Never envy, never slander, never despair,
wish well to all, work hard and hope.

And he always followed his own advice.

I asked Anna Sedláková if she would write something too. She said she would be pleased to. She took the scrapbook home with her and when she had finished her contribution, asked me if she could bring it to our house. Of course I agreed, feeling quite overwhelmed by the honour.

When she rang at our door my heart was thumping with excitement, as if God himself were on the doorstep.

She was sitting in Father's armchair when she handed me the book. I thanked her over and over again. She had written in her calligraphic hand the following verses:

Life hastens on, and we are scarce aware
how, pace by pace, we too are hastening.
Today, tomorrow, both evaporate
as winter follows summer, autumn spring.

The world around is changing at every step
and we ourselves strange alterations know;
smiling today, tomorrow we shed tears,
and where flowers bloomed at dawn, the night brings snow.

One more year passes and we shall forget,

and feel the frozen dew of indifference
behind us, like a gravestone, earthward fall.

These things alone – the nursery tales we learned,
and those dear ones who loved us – these alone
always, and gratefully, we shall recall.

Very soon after this Anna Sedláková was transferred to a post elsewhere and I never saw her again. I missed her greatly and will never forget her.

6

The Jewish holidays

There were only a handful of Jewish families in our town and the surrounding area, living the same kind of life as everyone else. They all had their own jobs, offices, businesses, farms. Their children went to the same schools, spoke Czech, joined in Sokol gymnastics and had lived on Czech soil since time immemorial. They did not feel superior or inferior to the rest. They didn't follow Jewish dietary laws; they ate the same food and drank the same beer.

It was only the religious holidays that were different. They did not have Christmas trees nor go to church for midnight mass nor join in the Corpus Christi procession – except for me, who went secretly because I enjoyed it as a piece of theatre – but they observed their own Jewish holidays. There was one around Easter time, the Pesach, and in the autumn was the Jewish New Year and Yom Kippur, the Day of Atonement. Each one had something to do with food, and that was all they meant to me at the time. Either there was a great feast or nothing at all. Or a fast; on Yom Kippur we weren't allowed to eat or drink anything for twenty-four hours. I wasn't clear why and I used to sneak back home for a bite.

For me it was a different kind of holiday. Our Katty and Anca always baked potato fritters in the oven that day, red and crunchy, something we never had at any other time. I looked forward to the Day of Atonement all year. There was no synagogue in our town, only a little prayer room. This was a simple first-floor room, set aside and furnished for prayer. There was a raised desk on which the *torah* lay open between two scrolls and was read from in Hebrew. The visiting rabbi used to point to the words with a long silver pointer in the shape of a hand. In between readings he would sing sad melodies I had never heard, in a language I didn't know, quite different from anything I had come across in school. Behind the desk was a casket with a heavy curtain embroidered in gold and silver thread. On either side in front of the platform stood a row of benches; men sat on the left, women on the right.

Grandfather, as one of the older generation, observed all these festivals scrupulously. He went to the prayer room wearing a *talles*, a white shawl with black stripes, over his shoulders. And he really did pray.

Father kept the holidays too, not so much for tradition's sake as Grandfather did, but more out of respect for him. Or perhaps they meant something to him. I don't know.

For Mother, the Jewish holidays were like two milestones dividing the calendar: one in the spring, one in the autumn. Those were when you did the big washing and cleaning and got ready for the major feast. On festival days she went to the prayer room, but more as a social event than out of piety. She had her prayer book open on the rest in front of her. It was supposed to be read Hebrew-style, from right to left. But the womenfolk just gossiped, about children and household matters, I suppose.

At Yom Kippur, when everyone was meant to be fasting, it was the custom to take into the prayer room for each mother a fresh apple stuck with cloves to make it smell nice. The idea was to sniff them to avoid fainting from hunger.

That was something else I looked forward to each year, so that I could make pretty patterns with the cloves.

My only objection to the Jewish holidays was that I wasn't allowed to go to school on those days, and had to wear my best clothes, Sunday clothes, even if it was a weekday. This made me feel excluded and I felt I was being pointed at and told to stand apart, all for no reason. When my schoolmates passed by they stared at me as if they had never seen me before, and I didn't belong amongst them – even though I was the same person I was the day before. I hated this invisible gulf separating me from the others.

One day Father announced that we were going to have a motorcar. That was still a rarity. People travelled by train or bicycle, or went on foot. But buy a car he did, a brand new Peugeot. There it was, standing quietly in front of the house, painted green, with huge mudguards and mica windows that were hard to see through. Father was wearing a chauffeur's uniform bought for the purpose, including large goggles tied with elastic, and big chauffeur's gloves with cuffs up to the elbows.

One had to turn a crank to start the motor.

The whole family set forth in style for a Sunday outing. We had been thinking what fun it would be to drive out into the countryside in our own car. But we didn't get far. It started raining, and then suddenly the whole car lurched over to one side. A wheel had come off and rolled away into a potato field.

We all had to get out. Jirka and I went to look for the wheel among the potatoes. Meanwhile Father was bent double, like a mushroom picker, searching the road for the lost nuts and screws so he could put the wheel on again once Jirka and I had found it. There was no one else on the road. In the end Father managed more or less to put the car together. We got in and drove home again, dirty and sopping wet.

Mother complained that there'd been no need to drive anywhere at all. Her remark quite ruined Father's pleasure in the new car. Ever since then I have distrusted cars and preferred to walk everywhere, or go by train for longer distances.

———✳———

Life went on in a calm and orderly way, like a river flowing through a gently hilly landscape with no sudden bends or rapids. Sometimes it went through woods, sometimes between flowery meadows. Our daily life had the same sort of regular rhythm. For Father it was mostly business and travelling around; for us children school and holidays and fun in the country; for Mother the household, shopping, cooking, twice-yearly cleaning, and the Great Wash once a month.

This last was a great affair that took a whole week, and had a special routine. One started by hiring a washerwoman, who installed herself in the underground scullery, from which steam spewed into the courtyard all day. She was a professional and knew what she was doing.

There was any amount of laundry, several basketfuls. First everything was soaked, then scrubbed on washboards in wooden tubs, which had been drawn tight the day before so that they didn't leak. Meanwhile, water was heating in the boiler. The next stages were rinsing, bluing and finally, starching.

The biggest problem was finding space to hang it all out to dry. This depended on the weather. If it was clear, clothes lines would be stretched out across the yard and the laundry hung up with pegs. But it could happen that the Great Wash fell on a day when it was raining non-stop. Then everything had to be taken up, a basketful at a time, to the third floor and hung between the attic rafters. There it would take several days to dry. In the winter the whole lot used to freeze stiff.

Sometimes the day started with promising sunshine, until the sky suddenly darkened and there was a downpour. Then everyone in the house had to rush out, help take the clothes down from the lines and carry them up, load by load, to the attic.

Washing and drying the laundry were only the first stages of this military-style operation. After the dry clothes had been taken down and laid in the baskets, they were brought into the kitchen and sorted out like components on a production line. Bed linen, such as sheets, pillowcases and duvet covers, went in one pile. Bath, hand and kitchen towels and handkerchiefs went in another. Then came men's shirts, then tablecloths, napkins, doilies and so on. Mother had her system and was very methodical about everything domestic. Before any ironing was done, the laundry had to be sprinkled. Large items like sheets and tablecloths were pulled out so that the edges and corners met with geometric precision. Then they were put through the mangle – two rollers turned manually with a huge handle. Ironing was done on two ironing boards and a large table. Mother, Katty and Anca all did the ironing together. Sometimes I joined in too, if Mother told me to drop everything else and "get some practice".

The iron was hollow with a little flap on the top that closed with a hook. It was heated with a lump of gun-metal, that first had to be made red-hot over a blazing stove and then fed into the iron with a pair of tongs. So that the laundry didn't scorch, one first had to try the iron out on a piece of newspaper. There was a cardboard pattern for every item of clothing so that each could be folded into the right shape before being tied up with lilac-coloured satin ribbon. All the washing ended up snow-white and smelling of lilac and fresh breezes. Before things were put into the chests of drawers they were laid out in regular rows. On ironing day the kitchen looked like a parade ground.

7

Yugoslavia

When I was eleven I started grammar school, which brought fresh worries: more subjects, less time for playing out of doors, and a new disturbing element. There were boys in class for the first time. This upset our equilibrium. Each of us was enamoured with one of them. Or as it was usually put, "*She's* barmy about Tom, *she's* barmy about Dick," and so on.

We either sat giggling on the benches or sent each other secret notes. It was all very exciting and schoolwork suffered accordingly. To be escorted home by one's chosen gallant was pure ecstasy. On Sunday mornings we dolled ourselves up to parade around the main square in the hope that he would appear too. There was a garrison in the town, and if junior, or even senior, officers turned up, the promenade became very colourful and thrilling, with much exchanging of coquettish glances.

———✳———

It was very soon that I fell deeply in love for the first time. I was just twelve. During the summer holidays Father dispatched Jirka to a scout camp, while Mother, my sister and I were sent to Novi on the Yugoslav coast. The Adriatic

Sea – not just a fishpond in the countryside! I couldn't wait to see it. Mother got the local seamstress, Mrs Kuchlerová, to make us some beach outfits, which we called "beach pyjamas" because they looked so much like normal pyjamas. Two pairs for each of us, one pale blue and one pink. That was the fashion.

Having them made was torture. I had to stand still so long, I felt I would pass out each time Mrs Kuchlerová slowly pinned the sleeves onto my clothes, marked the length with chalk and fitted the sailor-boy collar. So my visits there put me off the holiday and the seaside idea altogether.

We went by train, a very long journey. I had a window seat. Suddenly in the distance I had my first glimpse of blue sea. A mysterious new world now opened up for me. We stayed in a lovely big hotel with a room and balcony overlooking the sea. We had our own cabin on the beach. The sand was so hot that we had to wear beach shoes the whole time. The water was warm, the sea stretched out forever and I couldn't take my eyes off it.

There was a beach promenade over a kilometre long in front of the hotel. All the guests walked there every evening. My sister Lydia, who was only six, walked with my mother, but I was twelve and walked by myself. I had other things on my mind.

There was a young boy going up and down the promenade, with a red scarf around his neck attached to a large wooden tray laden with variously coloured goodies: candied fruit, toffee apples and lollipops. As he sold them to the visitors he recited strange rhymes in a language that sounded like Czech, but wasn't. It was a kind of song with rhythm, but no tune. He had black eyes and a dusky complexion. I fancied him terrifically. Rajko was his name.

Once when Mother stayed behind in the hotel I sneaked out onto the promenade to help Rajko sell his wares.

I learned his words by heart and had them so pat that no one could tell I wasn't a native.

We would walk along side by side, singing:

Mindoli mandoli
karameli
kysely vesely
london bombon
ris paris
aaafrika paaaprika
cuc na bidýlku ...

Lots of people came up to buy and Rajko's sales spiralled.

One day he took me by the hand and walked quietly across the sand with me to the water's edge and back again. There was a great white ship on the horizon and I imagined us sailing away on it one day, into the unknown. Just the two of us.

My dream of bliss sank below the horizon along with the white ship, for next day Mother, my sister and I were on our way home again. The new school year was about to start. But Yugoslavia had been paradise.

8

The piano

By the time we got back from our holiday I felt so sophisticated. Vera and I decided it was high time we learned to smoke and behave like grown-ups. "Let's have a go," we agreed.

At the first opportunity, when our parents went off to Prague for a couple of days, we decided to take action. We bought a packet of Vlasta cigarettes at U Sýkoru, the nearby kiosk. That was ten cigarettes, more than enough for us. To create a cosy atmosphere we settled down in the little room in our house, drew all the curtains, lowered the lights to make it like a night club and put a Ramona waltz on the gramophone. Then we wound it up and put on the needle.

Sentimental music filled the room. Solemnly lighting our first cigarettes, we crossed our legs and felt like film stars, albeit coughing film stars. At the end of her first cigarette Vera was sick. But we had passed our first test of maturity.

In the new school year I started taking piano lessons. We had an old Hayek grand piano at home that had been part of Mother's dowry. No one played it. It was out of tune and some of the keys had gone yellow like old teeth.

As luck would have it, there was a German piano teacher in our town, a Professor Kurzová, who went to Prague twice a week to teach at the Conservatoire. She was the wife of a local doctor.

Professor Kurzová only accepted a small number of pupils, but she agreed to take me on. There were two Förster pianos in her place, an upright for students and a grand for herself. She was a follower of the old German classical music school and taught accordingly. Technique was the be-all and end-all. Scales – upward and downward – in all positions and modes: major, minor, chromatic. She was very strict, but I enjoyed the lessons and spent hours practising. Though I made good progress, Mother had no high opinion of my musical ambitions. Every time I sat down to practise she would drive me away, shouting, "There you go tinkling the ivories again. Why don't you darn some socks or go through your drawers? That'd be more useful."

But I had an answer to that. So as not to have to give up practising I put on woollen gloves and carried on, hoping my mother wouldn't hear me.

I had a lot of backing from my father, though. He was very musical and had perfect pitch. He played the violin excellently without sheet music, just by ear. He often came up behind me at the piano, picked up his violin and played duets with me. That was a real joy.

Sometimes I would tell my father that this or that piece was too hard for me to learn. He always cut me short. "Never say something's too hard to learn. Tell yourself that if a circus elephant can learn to walk on bottles, you can train yourself to do anything. If you really want to, that is."

Father always looked on the bright side of everything and was wonderful at telling stories about his travels or his experiences in the army in World War I.

There was one moment in the day when we were all

together: at precisely seven o'clock at the dinner table. Nobody was allowed to miss it and punctuality was the law. This was the occasion for Father to tell his stories. He put a lot of humour into them, as well as pieces of wise advice, often aimed at me. I was his favourite, partly, no doubt because I reminded him most of his beloved Betty. People often used to say, "Just like her mother!" and look in my direction.

"Never try to have too much of anything in life!" he said on one occasion. "Just see that you have what you need and a little more. That's good enough. When you die, all you will take with you is what you've given to other people."

Another time he said to me: "You'll meet all sorts during your life. Form your own judgement about them – not by how they earn their money but by what they spend it on."

In my case his words fell on fertile soil. Even if I didn't understand them at the time, they germinated like seedlings and came into flower later.

"Look around you, observe, learn and educate yourself. We are put here to develop and perfect ourselves as much as we can, not to climb social ladders. They don't lead anywhere. Remember, if a dwarf climbs even to the highest mountain top, he is still a dwarf."

In his own business, too, Father was courageous and full of enterprise. Sometimes he had ideas that were well ahead of his time. He got interested, for example, in the possibility of producing petrol from our native coal. The more he thought about it, the more convinced he was that there were ideal conditions in our country for achieving this.

Why not start with the huge deposits around Moravian Ostrava, near the Polish borders? He probed and probed.

He who seeks shall find. A few other specialists were needed, and soon enough they turned up. One was a first-rate Berlin research chemist, another a well-known Prague barrister. All three were convinced of the merits of the scheme and felt sure this revolutionary new source of petrol would come into being.

They formed their own company, with Father as the main source of finance. Mother was against it. She said it would lead nowhere and Father ought to forget it and stick to his own trade – steel.

The plan was sound in theory, but impracticable, and the company went bust. The German chemist escaped back to Berlin. The Prague barrister shot himself, and Father lost a lot of money.

"I told you so," said Mother.

But he never despaired, or even repented. "That's how things go in life. If you take risks you must count on sometimes losing."

He threw himself into his normal business again and soon recouped his losses.

9

Dancing classes

During our teenage years we loved wandering in the nearby woods with their smell of moss and fungi, and carpets of blueberries and wild strawberries in the sun-warmed clearings. We would lie in the soft grass and listen to the birds making conversation in the treetops. The world was lovely, life was safe and went merrily on its way. On top of that, we had started dancing lessons so as not to be behind when we grew up and became ladies. All was excitement and preparation.

Materials had to be bought. Ribbons. Dresses had to be sewn. New shoes tried on. New hairdos: they were the worst. Mother took me to the hairdresser on the town square, Mrs Hejrovská, to have my hair waved. First she wound it around little tongs that had been laid on a paraffin stove to be heated up. The hairdresser tested their temperature first on newspaper.

They were so hot the paper always burned. Having made tight curls all over my head, she then took the big tongs for squeezing the hair into waves. One wave to the left, one to the right, one to the left again, and so on. During this process she held the hair with a large comb, pressed it into waves with the tongs and finished the coiffure with a mass of combed-out curls.

As my hair was naturally straight and thick, these sets

never lasted long. Mother decided it would be best if I had a perm. This was a lengthy and rather frightening procedure. First they wound my hair around little rollers. I could see something hanging down from the ceiling like a medieval instrument of torture, waiting to be used on me. It had thin rubber cables, like black snakes tipped with clips, all hanging from a candelabra-like ring. The clips were attached to the rollers with my hair wound around them, and then the electricity was switched on. I sat paralysed in my chair, plugged into the ceiling and abandoned to my fate.

If something caught fire, I thought, I wouldn't be able to free myself and I should burn to cinders. Various other disastrous variations flitted through my head. After a long wait they released me from the instruments of torture and took off the clips and rollers. Behold, I was a new person with a frizzy sheepskin on my head. I'm not sure if it had come out as Mother had intended, but that's what it looked like.

On the following evenings I went to the dancing classes held in the Great Sokol Hall. In one corner there were boys standing in tight suits with polished boots and hair stuck down with brilliantine. The girls were in another corner. We all eyed each other to see who had the prettiest dress and who was wearing a bow. The mothers and chaperones sat on chairs along the wall, watching us critically and waiting to see which boy would come to sweep their treasure away.

Mr Kalivoda, the dancing master, arranged us in pairs and the music struck up. He introduced us to various combinations of step and rhythm: foxtrot, slow waltz, tango. We skidded on the polished parquet floor and the boys trod on our new shoes. By the end of the evening one could see the outlines of their sweaty hands on the backs of our new dresses. The dancing classes culminated in an elaborate ball – which meant one more dress – and then the season was over.

10

A trip to Prague

Except for her sister in Kolín, Mother's entire family lived in Prague. Twice a year we journeyed to the capital to visit Grandmother.

Great excitement, busy times. The day before the journey was spent feverishly preparing food to take with us so that we wouldn't die of hunger on the way. We took a hamper full of cutlets and gherkins, hard-boiled eggs, buttered rolls, fruit and lemonade. We had to get up before daybreak as the distance to Prague was so great – more than seventy kilometres. My brother, sister and I stood to attention on the platform in our Sunday best, while Mother bought the tickets at the counter.

The stationmaster, a stocky little man with a weedy moustache, paced up and down the platform holding a huge bell and watching for the first sign that the Prague train was approaching. As soon as he saw steam above the trees he clutched his bell tight and reeled off the names of all the stations as far as Prague.

When the train arrived we climbed up the steep steps, Mother found a free compartment and immediately we were told to eat. The train had its own special smell of soot and cigarette smoke and we were not allowed to have the windows open in case we got smuts in our eyes. After half an hour we reached Beroun, where platform vendors were crying "Hot frankfurters, lemonade, newspapers!" and Mother bought each of us a roll and frankfurter. After Beroun I was always sick.

When the Smíchov tunnel approached we had to prepare to get out by putting on our jackets and, worst of all, our gloves. These white gloves were made from sharp cotton needlepoint and were uncomfortably tight around the fingers. I hated Smíchov. Then came Prague – the Wilson Central Station – with all its noise and bustling crowds, luggage, porters and newspaper vendors. Prague belonged to the outside world.

At Grandmother's the table was already set with a coffee service and in the middle, awaiting us, stood a *bábovka* cake sprinkled with sugar and set with almonds.

All Mother's relations were there, housed together in a great four-storeyed building on Týnská Street, one family to each floor.

There were three boy cousins of our own age – Harry, Péta and Bedrich. They had brought their own toys and we played all kinds of games together while the grown-ups chatted about family matters and other adult topics.

The next day we had to accompany Mother to the Boulevard coffee house on Wenceslas Square, where all the other aunts were gathering. There were at least five of them seated at a single round table on the first floor behind a window, like a tableau. They always greeted me with the same words:

"My, hasn't she grown! So what's new at school?"

I never knew what to say to that. I was much more interested in what was going on around me. The coffee house was humming with noise and movement, people coming and going, talking and laughing. Frock-coated waiters threaded their way through clouds of cigarette and cigar smoke, balancing trays of coffee and cakes, canapés, and other delicacies. A small pageboy in red uniform, with gold buttons and a little fez on his head tied with elastic under his chin, walked between the rows of tables holding up a name card on a stick and announcing that the person in question had a telephone call:

"*Doktor Neuman k telefonu! Doktor Neuman k telefonu!*"

And a moment later he would be calling for someone else.

If it was raining on our way back we could see the flashing neon lights of the evening paper *Vecerni Ceské Slovo* reflected in the asphalt of Wenceslas Square, as the letters chased across the façade of the newspaper building, vanishing and reappearing endlessly. Cars, lights, people, movement, shop windows, trams, splendid buildings, the Vltava River and the Hradcany castle looming over it – Prague was one big dream. A world of its own, quite different from the one we knew at home.

11

Political clouds begin to gather

Reports had begun to filter in from Germany – a country as distant from our own as if it were on another planet – about the new political order being established there by the Chancellor, one Adolf Hitler. The radio had broadcast several of his demagogic speeches. He sounded to us like any other fanatic, bawling and threatening. His followers and his brown-uniformed storm troops multiplied day by day, but nobody we knew took him seriously. Mother hated listening and Father totally ignored him.

"No need for us to bother about him," he said. "We're no longer part of the Austro-Hungarian Empire. Although we understand and speak German, this is not Germany. Hitler is in Germany and this is the Czechoslovak Republic. President Masaryk is in charge here and no country in the world has a better statesman at the helm."

Life went on as usual and people forgot about Germany again.

One Easter Saturday I was in a crowd in front of the Parliament building in Prague, waiting tensely for Papa Masaryk to appear. I had never seen him before, only his portrait that had hung in my elementary school and my grammar school, and graced every public building in the country. Just before midday there was a murmur in the crowd and then a shout of "Here he comes!"

And it really was he, President T.G. Masaryk himself in his familiar white suit, on horseback. He jumped down and ran as nimbly as a youngster up the front steps of the Parliament. I caught my breath, seeing him with my own eyes, our one and only Papa Masaryk, handsome as a living statue, and yet somehow unreal, visionary.

I wept with joy and excitement and knew it was an experience no one could ever rob me of. I felt privileged above the citizens of all other nations in being a child of Masaryk's Republic.

———✦———

Soon afterwards we became accustomed to seeing another portrait alongside Masaryk's – that of Eduard Beneš, who became the new president of the Republic when the ageing president retired. Nothing had been lost, quite the opposite. We had two strong watchdogs now, one in the forefront and one on guard behind. But on 14 September 1937, T.G. Masaryk died. Our whole nation wept over the loss of its great man – the President-Liberator. We all felt we would never see his like again.

We stood at the window of a flat near the Wilson Central Station and watched the train carrying his coffin – on a low pedestal in an open wagon – on its way out of Prague to his last resting place in Lány. As it passed close to us people knelt and some prayed, not only for his soul, but for our country and its fate. When his coffin left, it was as if the last days of free Czechoslovakia were departing too.

12

Fred Astaire – *You are my lucky star*

Little by little, my life began to be influenced by seemingly far-fetched and quite disconnected events.

Hollywood had released a new film, a musical, *Broadway Melody*. It included a number of catchy tunes and songs like *You are my lucky star*, which quickly became very popular.

There was not, could not be, the slightest link between me and that film. And yet, life moves in mysterious ways. We were on another of our annual visits to Grandmother in Prague. Cousin Bedrich was boasting that he had a brand new gramophone record with songs from the latest film. Yes, *Broadway Melody*.

"Let's hear it!" we all cried.

He put the record on the machine and dropped the needle. Fred Astaire's resonant voice filled the room: "You are my lucky star ..."

Without knowing a word of English I found the song fascinating. Bedrich had to play it for me over and over until I knew it by heart, from start to finish. I had a knack for languages and just as I was able to pick up Yugoslav, I could pick up English. I sang it as I heard it, phonetically, with no idea of the meaning. To my ears the opening words sounded like some imaginary Czech words, *Jú ... ár ...*

majlakista on the grammatical model of *hokejista*, hockey player, but so what? This is the way it has to sound if it's in English, I decided. And that was that. The thought suddenly came into my mind, almost like a premonition, as I listened to that song, that I had to learn English, come what may.

The plan had no practical value at the time. We all talked Czech at home and at school and I didn't know a soul in England, so what use could the language be to me? Yet this inner voice kept whispering to me that one day I should need it.

When I got back home and started at the grammar school again, all thoughts of English were forgotten. Meanwhile the air was full of broadcasts from Germany; Hitler's speeches grew ever more hysterical and threatening, and he now had half his countrymen behind him. Every broadcast by the leader was followed by long-drawn-out calls of "*Sieg Heil! Sieg Heil! Sieg Heil!*" "Salute Victory! Salute Victory! Salute Victory!" repeated endlessly.

Mother began to be very anxious, but Father always calmed her down. "Hitler can't do us any harm," he would say. "And if he had the cheek to try, he'd be in for a surprise. We've got a magnificently trained army, strongly fortified frontiers and a binding treaty of mutual assistance with lots of friendly nations. So keep calm and don't panic."

13

The 1938 holidays and Dr Mandelík

That year we didn't arrange any big journeys and the summer holidays were divided between picking wild strawberries and mushrooms in the woods, swimming in the river and playing tennis at the Áleje.

It was stifling hot and the roads were dusty.

Mother decided to send me off for a fortnight to her sister Irma in Kolín, east of Prague. That was something to look forward to. My cousins Pavel and Vera took me to the baths on the river Elbe. After swimming we spent the rest of the afternoon playing tennis at their club.

On one occasion I was the last to leave and wasn't sure how to get back to their house. A strange man came up to me after he had finished his game. He struck me as pretty old, about twenty-eight, with auburn curls and spectacles. Seeing me standing at the gate looking so helpless, he asked if he could drive me home. I said thank you, and certainly, I'd love him to. His car was a big black Hudson and I was home in no time. I had to promise him that we would go to Spa Podebrady together the next day for "Five o'clock Tea" with dance music. It all sounded very enticing and romantic. Aunt Irma saw us get out and when I arrived at her house she was beside herself with excitement.

"Do you realise who it was who drove you home?"

"One of the locals," I answered. "He didn't even tell me his name."

"But that was Dr Mandelík!" she burst out breathlessly.

Her voice was trembling with awe and admiration as if I had been escorted by the heir to some royal throne, and looked reproachfully at this Cinderella who wasn't even aware what an honour she had been paid.

The Mandelíks were a grand and wealthy family from Ratbor near Kolín whom everyone knew and looked up to as the local gentry. Their sugar factories supplied the whole republic, and foreign customers too. Originally, there had been three brothers, one of whom lived with his family in Ratbor and organised production. Another was in Prague in charge of distribution and a third in Paris.

The Ratbor brother, Otto, and his wife Olga, had a daughter, Hana, and a son, Bernard. He was my new chauffeur. Bernard already had a doctorate in chemistry and was supposed to take over the production technology and the refineries some day. They lived in a grand mansion.

There was a very tense atmosphere in Aunt Irma's household that evening on account of my new acquaintance. She lost no time in ringing my mother to tell that her daughter had made a good match – as if it were all settled and despite the fact that I didn't even know the gentleman's name. "Well, well, who would have thought she was up to it?" my mother retorted, with mild irony.

All the same, she could not resist passing on the family news immediately to other relations and enjoying a little glory as mother of the bride-to-be.

The intriguing news caused no little stir; everyone embroidered it somewhat, and within twenty-four hours it was being repeated as a *fait accompli*. "Have you heard the latest? Zdenka is going to marry one of the Mandelíks!"

The next day, Mr Mandelík came to pick me up in

his black car to take me to Podebrady, just as he had said. As soon as we were seated he solemnly presented me with a large box of chocolates. I was rather alarmed in case he should expect some mark of favour in return; I was only sixteen and had no experience with older men. But he didn't ask for anything. When we got to Podebrady, he treated me to tea and cake and drove me home again.

I was only due to stay another five days at Aunt Irma's. He came two more times and drove me around the neighbourhood. He talked about his family and his work. On the way home he laid his hand on my knee. Something twitched inside me and I knew I shouldn't have accepted those chocolates. When I got home Father took me aside and gave me some solemn advice.

"You can have everything you want in life," he said. "It's all spread out in front of you, like goods on a table. Just take what you like. But don't forget one thing. As soon as you pick it up, whatever it is, there is a price tag underneath. And that's what you've got to pay."

He looked me straight in the eyes.

"So always weigh up carefully whether what you're so keen on is really worth the cost."

The new school year started and I was in my junior year in high school.

Dr Mandelík kept sending me long letters to the school, which I bragged about to the other girls, mainly because they had red sealing wax on the back, stamped with the family arms and monogram. He introduced me to the beauties of Czech literature and sent me books of poems – Frána Šrámek's *"Stríbrný vítr"* (*Silver Wind*), Víteslav Nezval's *"Sbohem a šátecek"* (*Goodbye and a Scarf*), and many others. I started to feel important, but not in love. In a detached way it was a flattering adventure, but I never dreamed of anything closer.

There were lightning flashes now from the direction of Germany. Hitler had annexed Austria in March of 1938 and fancied he wanted our Sudetenland region, the militarily significant mountainous area bordering Germany. At various times in history it had been under both German and Czechoslovakian rule. He said it was his by rights and he would take it by force if the Republic didn't cede it voluntarily. We didn't oblige. We mobilised, and the whole nation resolved to stand up against Hitler and his army. Father, like many other patriots, joined up as a volunteer.

Then, in late September 1938, came the Munich Agreement, in which Neville Chamberlain, along with France and Italy, thought they could avoid war by letting Hitler annex the Sudetenland. Czechoslovakia wasn't consulted. No one could believe that England and our other allies had betrayed us, feeding us to a hungry Hitler as a preliminary morsel.

We were caught in a trap. The frontier defences were laid open, the Germans grabbed the Sudetenland, and our soldiers, Father among them, came home crestfallen. The net tightened around us as the radio blared *Sieg Heil! Sieg Heil!* ever more loudly.

Yet everyday life still proceeded along its well-worn path.

One autumn day, when my parents happened to be in Prague, Dr Mandelík rang at the door. His black Hudson was standing in front of our house. Quite unprepared for such a visit, I was frightened out of my wits. How should I receive him? What should I offer him? How is one supposed to behave with gentlemen like him when they come to your home?

He saw my embarrassment and suggested we go to Prague for lunch.

All the way to Prague for lunch? To the world's metropolis? That was a place one only went to twice a year, for several days and only after thorough preparation. But to drive there just for lunch? He assured me it was nothing out of the way. So off we went, straight to the Vanha Grill, the most exclusive and fashionable fish restaurant in Prague. It was the first time I'd been there. My knees were trembling, and my hands even more, when the waiter laid out a whole series of forks and variously twisted knives, like surgeons' instruments, on the table in front of me.

To be on the safe side I said I didn't eat fish. But Béra (he wanted me to call him by the name his family used) assured me that they only served the best quality there, and ordered trout and mayonnaise for me. I just about managed to cope without mishap. The room was full of smart company and elegant women. I was anxious either to look like one of them, or not be there at all.

After lunch Béra suggested we went to the pictures. On the other side of Wenceslas Square was a cinema showing Disney's *Snow White and the Seven Dwarfs* – the first ever full-length cartoon film with all the drawings moving and dancing around like live figures. We had never seen anything like it before.

When it was over we got into his car and he drove me home as if it had just been around the corner. For Béra it was no big deal, but for me the day had been an unforgettable dream.

———✦———

Winter was setting in and the year would soon be over. Suddenly a bombshell dropped.

A printed invitation card arrived from Béra, asking me to spend Christmas Eve with him at the family estate in Ratbor. It was a great honour, but what to do? I was a little scared. What preparations could I make? What should I wear? What *did* people wear in those circles?

Mother decided that if a girl was to hold her own and make a proper impression on the Mandelík family, she would have to have a fur coat. She took me to the nearest large town and we went to a furrier. He laid out various samples, including black Persian lamb. Though my opinion wasn't sought, I rejected this on the grounds that I wasn't going to a funeral.

Finally Mother and the furrier settled on a reddish-beige muskrat. Admittedly, this fur was generally used for linings, but they agreed that a coat made from it would look youthful. We went several times for fittings and finally we could see a three-quarter-length fur coat emerging. Out of the pelts left over the furrier made me a little hat to wear, tipped forward in the fashion of the times. I was looking forward to going out in my new coat right away, but Mother wouldn't hear of it. "This fur coat is to wear on the visit to Ratbor, not out in the street."

So I carried it home in its box and hung it up in the cupboard like a good girl. Mrs Kuchlerová made me a few more smart dresses as well. In the end I was kitted out like someone going to parade in a fashion show.

There was a peculiar atmosphere now at Aunt Irma's in Kolín. Suddenly they were treating me like an honoured guest and admiring my new outfits. They bought me a huge bouquet of flowers to present to Béra's mother on arrival.

Béra picked me up in his car at the appointed time. My aunt's family bade me farewell as solemnly as if I were going as far as Australia. I sat down in the car with my flowers and agonised about what the evening ahead of me would bring.

Arriving in Ratbor, we first went up a sand-strewn drive through a little park before coming to a halt in front of the mansion. There was an entrance hall with a fountain in the middle and a leather bench running around it. Suddenly Béra was nowhere to be seen. I was faced with a butler who bowed, took not only the flowers from me but my fur coat as well, and then went off to put them down somewhere. A thought flashed through my mind: I mustn't ever tell Mother that none of the family had even seen the coat! The way it turned out, I thought, I could just as well have worn it around town, or even to school.

The butler came back and led me into the reception room. It was a large, beautiful, furnished drawing room with a Christmas tree in the right hand back corner, all decorated and reaching up to the ceiling.

The room was already crowded with elegant, sophisticated people – on the oldish side, by my standards – who stood around or sat in various armchairs chatting, some of them sipping drinks from little glasses, and generally behaving informally. A good noisy group.

Béra was still nowhere to be seen. Suddenly I saw the butler coming back with my flowers in a vase, which he set down in a prominent position.

No one took any notice of me or asked me about anything. There was one little girl playing under the Christmas tree. This was Nina, the daughter of Béra's sister Hana.

Suddenly there was a slight stir as the lady of the house, Mrs Mandelíková, appeared. She was wearing a dark, low-cut dress and had black hair piled high. She slowly descended the spiral staircase and greeted her guests.

What was I supposed to do? The flowers were in water. How could I give her them in the vase? Yet I had to do it somehow. With one bound I reached the table where they stood, grasped hold of the vase and ran up to the hostess. Mumbling my name or something, I handed her the flowers, vase and all. She was slightly taken aback, but said thank you and put them down again on the nearest table.

Everything so far had turned out quite contrary to what I was prepared for.

There was another room adjoining with a large white Bösendorfer piano in it, the lid already open. One of the guests left the others and sat down to play Chopin's Ballade in G minor, and, as an encore, the A major Prelude.

When he had finished everyone clapped politely, but I felt that I, as a budding pianist, had appreciated it the most. I knew how accomplished he must have been to play those pieces so well.

After this little concert, which was by way of an interlude, the butler came into the main room with two black-uniformed maids wearing spotless little white aprons and white lace caps, and set the scene for Act II. The entire partition wall of the drawing room now rolled back to reveal the dining room, a wondrous sight suggesting not so much a dinner table as a refectory board for twenty-four people with Yuletide decorations dazzlingly illuminated.

In the middle, on a white damask cloth stretching from end to end, was a long pile of Christmas twigs in which stood little coloured candle figures, a different figure at each place. One guest had a dwarf, another a toadstool and so on. There were heavy candlesticks on the table as well, with their own candles. Innumerable cut-glass goblets and silver cutlery glittered in the candlelight.

I was scared to see how many different knives and forks of all shapes and sizes were lying on either side of the pile of plates in front of me. I just couldn't think of food. Béra was sitting opposite me and had no idea of my ignorance and insecurity: I was so afraid of committing some dire *faux pas* in the course of the evening and ending up as a dreadful failure among all these strange people.

Before the meal started, a telephone rang in the reception room. It was a friend of the family calling from Paris to wish them all a merry Christmas. It struck me as the very height of poshness to be rung up all the way from Paris. Anyway, we sat down to eat.

Mrs Mandelíková sat at the head of the table, with Mr Mandelík senior, the sugar baron, at the opposite end. Once we were in our places the staff started bringing the food around. There was gleaming white pike with mayonnaise on long silver platters. The butler first offered it to the hostess, who cut off a small slice with a silver knife and put it on her top plate. Then he went around all the other ladies in strict order according to their personal and family rank, and only afterwards started serving the gentlemen. Etiquette was very strict.

One course followed another: fish, soup, roast, poultry with green vegetables and sautéed new potatoes. Finally came chestnut purée with whipped cream and Christmas pastry. Everything was served with various wines. It was these that brought about my downfall. I wasn't used to alcohol and thought it rude ever to refuse.

No one had warned me. After the meal some of the guests withdrew to the smoking room, a cosy little place with brown wooden panels and little red leather armchairs. Béra invited me to follow him there. My head was already spinning as we went. Then more alcohol was passed around. I am told I was very skittish and talked to all the gentlemen. I don't recall that. All I remember is someone offering me a glass of brandy. That was my final undoing. The last moments of my visit to the Mandelíks are hazy. One of the guests drove me home, apparently, but I can't even remember that. I was lost to the world.

Aunt Irma and her whole family had stayed up to hear my report about the evening in Ratbor, but they couldn't get a word out of me. I dropped straight into bed.

By the morning I had sobered up and reality began to dawn on me. My introduction to the Mandelík family had proved a fiasco. Instead of admiration I had earned a bad name. I think I'll keep quiet about all that, I said to myself, and put it down to experience. Next time I won't touch any alcohol.

So I erased all acquaintance with Dr Mandelík from my mind. Ah well, I thought, it hasn't hurt me. Soon I will be off home and going back to school. I'll never say a word about it to Mother; she'd only be cross that she'd had the fur coat made for me for nothing.

I wasn't surprised that Béra didn't even ring up the following day. Just as well; I wouldn't have known how to apologise. And I didn't want to invent any transparent excuses. Best to drop it. It was all over. Full stop.

However, the day before I left Aunt Irma's, Béra did ring after all, and came to pick me up. I was grateful that he didn't say a word about Christmas Eve or my visit. All he wanted to tell me was that he was going to Paris in the new year to work with his uncle for three months. Then he gave me a hug and a goodbye kiss. And so we parted, going our separate ways. Though we didn't realise it, both of us were embarking on new stages of our lives, he in Paris and me in an unexpectedly different direction.

14

The German occupation

Father woke us up with a shout. "Quick, children, come to the window, all of you! Right away!"

It was only six in the morning. I wondered sleepily what on earth could be so important as to make Father wake us so early.

There was no brass band coming down the street. Whenever one did, Father always used to join in, picking up a broomstick for a baton and marching around the room like a military band conductor. If anyone was playing "The Radecky March" he could never resist it.

But there was no music this time. It was a miserable winter's day outside, raining with a bit of snow. A day like any other.

Wednesday, 15 March 1939.

Father's voice was trembling as he called again: "Come and look out of the window."

We opened the dining room curtains and through the second floor window saw an amazing sight: the German army. It was like a flood rolling down the street. Men on motorcycles, in strange uniforms and iron helmets, were hurtling out of the west in rows and columns, heading towards Prague. It sounded like the roar of an earthquake outside. No one spoke. I felt a chilling premonition of some unknown evil awaiting us.

Forget appeasement and the Sudetenland. Hitler wanted all of Czechoslovakia and he was taking it.

Apart from the invaders there was not a soul on the street. Only here and there could we see people standing at their windows, gazing with horror at the disaster that was overtaking our nation. There seemed no end to the motorised columns; they came in hundreds, perhaps thousands. We rushed to the radio to hear the announcer, with trembling voice, urging the public to keep calm and warning against any form of resistance. Everyone should stay indoors if possible, and the schools would be closed that day.

This was the only good news of the day for me: no school. We were due for a geography test on the Sahara. I'd done no homework and would have been quite at a loss if I'd been called on. This made me feel a little better.

The radio went on: "Await further announcements." We squatted around and waited. After about an hour came the nerve-racking news that the German army had reached Prague and occupied the presidential Hradcany Castle. It was hard to imagine, but everyone realised that this meant the end of the freedom we had known.

Mother was shivering with cold and had to put a warm wrap over her shoulders. Father looked pale. He had never expected this and was wondering what changes were to come, how soon, and how they would affect us. There were no answers, only speculation. Our resolve was to hold together as a family for as long as possible. Next day, we children went back to school and started preparing for the end-of-year exams that would soon be upon us.

Superficially, our lives still seemed unaffected. But a new element was creeping in that we had never known before. Fear. Uncertainty. What would happen next? What would become of us?

The start of the new school year, 1 September 1939, coincided with the German occupation of Poland and the declaration of the World War II. Meanwhile our own Republic had become a Reich Protectorate with a new government, which soon introduced race laws of the kind that Hitler had been mercilessly applying for years, but which we never believed could be put into practice in our country. Yet they were.

Overnight, the entire population was divided into two strictly separated camps – the Jews, and the others – as if, at the wave of a wand, we had turned into monsters and subhumans who were to be shunned by everyone else on penalty of imprisonment, or worse.

Next came the registration of Jews in every town, village, hamlet and isolated farm. Each was given a new identity card stamped *JUDE* – "JEW". A yellow star had to be sewn onto one's jacket so a Jew could be seen from afar and recognised as an enemy of the people.

Immediately after that the Germans started registering Jewish property, including businesses, offices, shops and bank accounts. Every Jewish owner had to surrender his business voluntarily and hand it over, with a signature of consent, to a German proxy and successor. He had to dismiss all his staff, even those with long years of service. Then he had to consign his domestic pets to collecting centres. The parting was painful.

Every door began to close. Signs appeared on cafés, restaurants and cinemas saying, "Jews unwelcome". One well-known shop put up a notice: "Dogs and Jews are not allowed in here". Ration cards were introduced, and notices posted that food would only be sold to Jews between three and four o'clock in the afternoon, when there was no more to be had.

More changes came thick and fast, starting with school expulsions. One fine day, Father was sent this letter from my grammar school:

By regulation No. 99761/40-J/l of 7Aug. 1940, the Ministry of Schools and National Enlightenment, in agreement with the Reichsprotektor, has decreed that with effect from the beginning of the school year no Jewish pupils will be admitted to Czech schools of any kind, and where Jewish pupils have been attending such schools they will be excluded from instruction from the start of the school year 1940/41.

I have to inform you accordingly that your daughter, Zdenka Fantlová, will no longer be a pupil at this institution.
[signed] Jan Hora, Headmaster.

So my case was settled. As I had finished my Junior year, I felt it was a shame I could not take my last year of school and graduate. My classmates were baffled.

"This is ridiculous. Perhaps it's a mistake. You'll soon see. He'll have second thoughts and you'll find yourselves back with us."

Ridiculous it certainly was, but it was no mistake. I was never allowed to go back. What now? Who should I turn to?

I thought about my options day and night. Suddenly the thought flashed through my mind: learn English! Remember Fred Astaire's *You are my lucky star*? I'd always wanted to master the language, and now I knew that I must. There was an English Institute in Prague where no race laws applied. They took anyone who wanted to learn English. So I decided I must get in there at all costs.

The first snag was Mother. As soon as I put it to her that I should like to study for another year, learn English at the Institute in Prague and live at Grandmother's, she turned the idea down flat.

"*You're* not going to stay in Prague. Girls only get corrupted there."

So that was that. There was no point arguing with her. I saw that I had to get around it some other way – through Father, in fact. But I needed a well-thought-out plan of action, so that he couldn't say no. Yes, a year in Prague would be just right.

I'll have to find someone whose opinion he respects, I mused. A teacher. But who? Ah yes, there was Father's close friend, a former professor of Latin at the high school. The moment of truth had come.

I went to see him. He was rather surprised at my visit but told me to sit down and tell him what was on my mind. I'd carefully prepared what I wanted to say and wasted no time. "I'm sure you'll understand. I've been thrown out of school because of the new race laws. I'm only seventeen and I'm anxious to complete my schooling and take another subject. The English Institute in Prague would surely take me on as a student. It would be no great financial burden on my father to pay the fees for one year. And I have a place where I could stay, my grandfather's behind the Old Town Square. Please talk to my father on my behalf. I would so love to have that year at the Institute."

I'm not sure if there were tears in my eyes, but I must have looked very wistful.

He was touched, and said: "You are quite right. A person of your age should spend all the time they can learning and improving themselves. I promise to talk to your father at the first opportunity, and I'll certainly urge him to let you go on with languages."

"Oh, thank you," I sighed, and walked home with a light step.

When Father came home the next day he settled down in his armchair, called me in and made a solemn proposal. "Now what would you think," he started, "about my sending you to the English Institute in Prague for a year so that you could learn another language? You're good at languages and you can't stay on at the high school."

I answered as casually as I could: "Mmm, why not? Sounds a jolly good idea. I won't be missing out on anything here, and it'll be another foreign language under my belt."

My strategy had paid off and I mentally thanked the old professor once again. Mother never dared to question anything my father suggested, so I went and packed my case. Two days later my father and I were on our way to Prague.

I felt happy and triumphant. It wasn't just that I was bound for the English Institute, but something more than that – something mysterious and fateful. I knew instinctively that I must learn this language that would one day save my life. I was not to know that the day would come exactly five years later.

15

Prague and The English Institute

Grandmother still lived in the family house on Týnská Street and the Institute was nearby on the Národní Trída.

I adored my daily walk through the narrow Prague streets, looking at the colourful façades and old family crests on the buildings, trying to imagine how people had lived there over the centuries and what actually went on in the ancient city. Even though I had to wear the yellow Jewish star on my jacket, no one bothered me. What I most enjoyed was walking on my own and exploring the byways on my way back from the Institute. I was truly in love with the city. The classes were from 9 a.m. to 1 p.m. The teachers were actual Englishmen and Englishwomen, from England. There was a Mr Henchman, a Miss Hinckley, and others. At that time, when there were so few foreigners around, it was like being in contact with a different world.

We had English grammars, read articles from English papers, practiced pronunciation, wrote dictations and were given homework to do.

Up to then, apart from listening to music, I hadn't known or heard a word of the language, but I loved the sound of it, worked hard and tried to be the best student. I looked forward to every class and nothing was too much for me.

Another student of my own age sat next to me, also from a provincial town, Nepomuk, and also expelled from school on racial grounds. Her name was Marta. We became fast friends and our destinies were so intertwined that later on, in quite unforeseeable circumstances, each of us was to save the other's life.

The two of us used to go on trips outside Prague, once by boat to Zbraslav, another time to Kokorín Castle. We would take the yellow stars off our coats and stride calmly into forbidden areas, going by tram, which was not permitted, and walking home after 8 p.m. when Jewish people were not even allowed on the streets. We were confident that no one in Prague would recognise us and by good luck we were never questioned. Poor Grandmother was scared stiff whenever I failed to arrive before the curfew began.

Marta and I both passed our final exams with distinction. I was particularly proud that my father wouldn't feel he had sent me to the Institute for nothing.

I went to see the old professor to show off, and to thank him for being the main agent of my success. He was pleased too, and congratulated me. Then in June the academic year ended and I had to go home again, where two events awaited me, one happy, one tragic.

16

My father is arrested by the Gestapo

After Prague, life at home seemed very boring, parochial and empty. The eight o'clock evening curfew was strictly observed and the Star of David always worn. This had to be immaculately sewn on, with no loose edges or points. I had to have a needle and thread always ready and make sure that the star on every coat was in perfect trim. The German screw was beginning to tighten. People were being arrested on the street with no reason given. We couldn't meet anyone, visit anyone or even stop and talk to them on the street.

The population of our town quickly polarised into two camps. There were those who spurned the German regulations and secretly helped us, especially in getting food outside the prescribed hours. And there were those who started collaborating with the Germans in the hope that they were finally onto a winning streak, that their time had arrived. They felt their duty was to spy on people and denounce them, in return for praise and sundry rewards from the Germans.

I stopped looking up my old friends to avoid causing problems for them and their parents; there were so many new eyes watching and ears listening. We had never distrusted people. We had always been able to talk openly, pass on information and share ideas without being afraid of anyone. But now we were always tight-lipped. An ugly monster had crept into our lives: fear of our fellow man. Who could tell if the butcher on the corner or the cigarette vendor opposite (even though he was a disabled World War I veteran), or our former washerwoman, or the innkeeper I used to fetch Father's beer from, might not be working with the Germans now, keeping an eye on us and watching for the slightest slip that could be reported to the appropriate quarters?

We did not have long to wait. People show their true colours in a crisis.

Under the anti-Semitic regulations we had to hand in our radio and rely on picking up chance fragments of information. One day a neighbour invited my father to come to his place and listen to the news from London in a Czech broadcast by the BBC. Listening to foreign stations was strictly forbidden and subject to grim penalties. Father accepted the invitation and went. He was excited to hear Jan Masaryk, the late President's son, addressing the Czechs and Slovaks from England. My father went around to that neighbour's place just twice. Shortly afterwards, when we were all sitting around the dinner table, about 8 o'clock in the evening, the doorbell rang – once, twice, three times – followed by a few sharp kicks on the door.

"*Gestapo! Aufmachen!*" "Open up!" came the order in German from outside.

My younger sister got up and opened the door. Three hefty SS men in uniform burst in, shouting wildly: "*Achtung! Aufstehen!*" "Attention! Stand up!"

We all had to get up from the table. They fell on Father like wild animals. One of them caught him by the collar, shook him and bellowed: "Name?"

Pale as he was, Father answered calmly with the German

pronunciation of his name, "Ernst Fantl."

"*Was?*" "What?", the SS man shouted, then told him how he should have answered – "Jew, Ernst Fantl!" – and hit him again.

There followed a scene of confused violence and screaming. I was sitting with my back to the wall and had to witness the whole hideous show.

"*Jetzt kommst du mit uns!*" "Now you come with us!" the officer in charge added menacingly. Two of the men seized Father by the shoulders while the third prodded and kicked him. Father staggered but managed to straighten up and ask in a quiet voice, "Can I take my coat?"

"*Los! Schnell!*" "Make haste!" One of them went to the bedroom with him and Father emerged with his coat on, holding his hat. Another German was standing astride at the open door in readiness. Father's face was grey, but before leaving the room he turned around, looked intently for a moment at each one of us in turn, as if to engrave our image on his memory, and then, in a low but steady voice, said:

"Just keep calm. Remember, calmness is strength."

And he raised his hat to us in silent farewell.

The Germans slammed the door closed and Father disappeared from our sight.

Mother fainted. When she came to, my brother and sister led her slowly to the bedroom and laid her on the bed.

I sat rooted to my chair like a marble statue, incapable of making any move. Once I had recovered from the shock my eyes fell on the table and the half-eaten meal. Throwing myself wildly on the food, I devoured every scrap I could find on the plates and dishes. I needed to get hold of something to save myself from drowning in the horror, confusion, fear and loss that I had just experienced.

When Mother came back into the dining room and saw what I had done, she rounded on me angrily, "How could you eat a single mouthful? It just shows you never loved your father!"

I was too shaken to explain to her that my feelings were the very opposite of what she thought.

None of us knew at the time why they had taken our father away, if indeed they had any reason. But we soon found out that a neighbour had informed on him for listening to the BBC broadcast.

We tried in vain to get some information about where they had taken my father that evening, or where he was now. Was he merely under interrogation, from which he might soon return? Or would we never see him again? It took us a long time, with much entreaty and bribing, to discover that he had in fact been taken to the Buchenwald concentration camp. We were allowed to send him a parcel of food, but never found out whether he got it. There was no communication.

Some months later we received a printed card saying that he was in Bayreuth, in Bavaria, in a prison for political offenders and had been given a twelve-year sentence for anti-state activity. After that there were brief messages from him at long intervals. Thus we learned that he was in a labour colony making paper bags. He was such a model inmate that he had been appointed leader of his group. I had a feeling that Father, lifelong optimist as he was, had adjusted himself to his conditions and was perhaps a little better off than if he had stayed in Buchenwald. So that was some comfort.

Life at home was more and more restricted. We felt like prisoners ourselves, anxiously speculating what changes might be in store for us and what would unfold. There was really no bright side to look on and we gradually succumbed to fatalism. *Que serà, serà.* What will be, will be. We had no other choice.

There was just one moment, before Father was taken away, when Britain offered to accept a certain number of refugees from the Protectorate as domestic servants. I announced at the dinner table that I could apply under this scheme – go to England and see what I could do next. Father turned to me curtly: "Get that out of your head! You're not going anywhere on your own. We are going to stay together, the whole lot of us, as we are."

And what had happened? We were already one fewer.

17

New love

Even before the Germans invaded, most of the Jewish families in the Sudeten borderlands had begun to move inland: some to Prague, some to provincial towns – wherever they had friends or relatives. These were in fact the first refugees to quit their homes out of fear of the Germans, leaving their property and livelihoods behind. They were like homeless exiles, relying on whoever would help them or be generous to them. They were generally regarded as second-class citizens. This hardly made for good cheer or optimism. What they didn't realise was that for them, as for all of us, there was much worse to come.

One family who moved into our town were the Levits from Tachov, oldish parents with a grown up son, Willi, a barrister, and a younger son, Arnošt, the same name as my father.

Arnošt was a striking young man with a fine physique, soft, dark hair and brown eyes that looked straight at you, glowing with courage. He was twenty-three. We met at a neighbour's for tea soon after his family arrived.

One glance at each other and lightning struck – it was love at first sight, and quite inevitable. From that day on we met as often as we could, mostly wandering in the woods, just us two. Arno, as I called him, used to come up to our window and whistle the theme from Dvořák's *New World Symphony*, our signature tune.

I always dropped everything immediately and ran outside to him. I couldn't whistle myself, so when I passed his house I had to ask a passerby to whistle the tune for me. Sometimes they obliged, sometimes they were reluctant – or perhaps they couldn't whistle either and didn't want to admit it.

We fell deeply in love, Arno and I, as if we had been waiting for each other all this time. For us, the world turned into a Garden of Eden. The German occupation vanished from our horizon. We could see nothing but one another, and felt no danger lurking ahead. If there was, what of it? Love would overcome all obstacles.

A good friend and former schoolmate of mine whom we bumped into on one of our country walks came up with this suggestion. "Look, I realise you're not supposed to be out after eight, so come to the mill where we live and you can stay with us overnight. Nothing to be afraid of. My people don't take any notice of German regulations anyway."

It sounded tempting, but not entirely safe, either for us or for my friend. However, the longing to spend a night together, anywhere, was stronger than our fear of any possible consequences. We settled for Saturday evening. We would come by bicycle. The mill stood on its own on a stream at the edge of a wood about an hour's walk from town.

But how was I to get out of the house? What could I tell Mother?

I confided the plan to my brother. We told Mother that only I and my brother would go and stay at the mill. My friend would find him some place to sleep. My brother saw the point and agreed.

We knew exactly what we were letting ourselves in for. Without official permission we weren't allowed anywhere outside the town boundaries. There would have been no point applying for permission. "On what grounds?" they would ask. So that was out. We had to risk going without permission, which meant that we also had to remove the Star of David from our garments. Both offences carried heavy penalties, but our minds were made up.

It was a lovely sunny day. Fortune was smiling on us. We put on clothes that didn't have the telltale stars on them. While we were still inside town we were scared that somebody might recognise us, notice that the stars were missing, and report us to the Gestapo. But nobody took any notice of us. Now we were out in the country and there was very little traffic. We were thinking our difficulties were over, when suddenly an open German army vehicle came around a bend with four uniformed SS men in it. We held our breath. Would they stop us? Would they ask who we were and where we were going? Would they ask to see our identity papers?

We were lucky, our guardian angels kept us from danger. The car passed close by us and drove on at high speed. Quaking at the knees, we decided to leave the main road and follow a narrow lane between fields. We knew the way: it would take a bit longer but it would be safer, so we calmed down and proceeded. We didn't realise that nothing in life is ever quite certain.

Suddenly a German officer appeared, cycling along the lane towards us. He came to a sudden stop, raised his arm and shouted "*Halt!*"

There was no escape. We thought our end had come. We stopped and jumped off our bikes. I went up to him to speak for the three of us. I looked him fearlessly in the face like someone who has nothing more to lose.

"How far is it to town from here?" he asked, in a quite normal tone.

Taking a deep breath so that my voice wouldn't shake, I said, "If you go this way," – and pointed – "you can get there in about half-an-hour. It's not far," I added genially, as if I were talking to a lost pilgrim.

"*Danke*," he saluted, and got on his bike and rode off. This time we had been really scared and had to sit down by the side of the road to recover our nerves.

Finally we reached our destination. The house and the mill stood in a sunny meadow by the forest and the river bubbled merrily as it passed over the mill wheel. Far and wide not a soul could be seen. It was like a storybook picture, a paradise for lovers. They offered us a small room with a tiny window, and the mill wheel turning just below. There was a straw mattress on the floor, a pillow and some rough blankets. The moon shone through the window.

The outside world vanished.

All we had was love – wild, eager, intoxicating, endless. Through the window came the sound of water and the scent of lime trees. Limbs intertwined. If only the night could go on forever. We promised each other eternal love and imagined our future life together, after the war, as soon as peace came.

The next day we rode home, still in a dream.

18

The Jewish transports

In the autumn of 1941, rumours began to circulate that in Prague lists were being drawn up of Jewish families earmarked for transportation to the East. Where in the East? No one knew. Reports from relatives in Prague became more frequent every day. The name Lódz, a town in Poland, cropped up; apparently a ghetto had been set up there to which transports from our country would be sent. No one was clear whether this was truth or speculation. We were all swathed in uncertainty about German intentions.

But there is no smoke without fire, and the stories turned out to be true.

All of a sudden human transports, a thousand people at a time, were being organised in Prague for dispatch to Poland. Every day we had news of people being summoned and of people who had actually been sent, friends and relatives of ours. Everyone knew it was the beginning of something indescribable, something we had always tried to believe would never happen in our country. Hitler's repeated threats to liquidate the Jewish race throughout Europe continued to dominate broadcasts from Germany. But as long as you lived at home in your own house, and slept in your own bed, you felt safe and "transport" was nothing more than a word. It conjured up no picture.

So far it affected only people in Prague, not us in the provinces. Perhaps it would never reach us. Drowning men clutch at any straw.

Late one evening our doorbell rang. My brother went to open the door. It was a good friend of my father's, a teacher born in the town. He lived near the woods. We let him in and shut the door quickly so that no one would know he had come.

"It's not looking too good for you people," he began. "They're already sending transports to Poland from Prague. Your turn is sure to come next. You'll have to leave everything behind. So if you've got anything you want kept safe, pack it up. I'll come for it tomorrow evening and hide it in our place. Then when the war's over you can pick it up from me. I was very fond of your father, you know."

There are always good people to be found, and quite a few turned up at this time. Quickly, we put a few pieces together, mainly family photographs, documents, things my mother had been slowly saving up as dowries for my sister, Lydia and me: bed linen, monogrammed kitchen towels, tablecloths and napkins.

We also took down from the dining room wall a painting of Blatná Castle that Father had been so fond of and used to gaze at. The place reminded him of his youth and his happy early days with his dear beloved Betty. We added the painting to our little collection. Otherwise we had no valuables left; Father's business and our bank accounts had already been confiscated.

The following day the teacher came as he had promised and drove away with our things under cover of darkness. The future that awaited us was gradually starting to take shape.

19

AK1 and AK2

The name Terezín – Theresienstadt to the Germans – a fortress town northwest of Prague, meant little to us at the time. Although it was well inside Bohemia, there was seldom occasion to mention this military stronghold. It was established by the Emperor Josef II between 1780 and 1790 and surrounded by high walls with small, well-fortified entrances.

But suddenly this little town came to the forefront and acquired quite a new reputation. News filtered through that it was being turned into an assembly camp for all the Jews in the country. We got out a map and looked to see in what direction Terezín lay from Prague. It didn't seem so horrible. If they evacuate us to that place, we pondered, we shall still be on Czechoslovak territory, still more or less home-based – just elsewhere, in a different town.

We didn't have long to wait before the first two transports, consisting of 2,000 young men left from Prague. They were dubbed AK1 and AK2 – AK for *Arbeitskommando*, labour detachment. Their assignment was to do construction work that would prepare Terezín to accommodate the many Jews who were going to be sent there. That was in November 1941.

This new development struck at the heart of our family. My cousin Bedrich, the one who had introduced me to the

Fred Astaire number, *You are my lucky star*, that was to play such a crucial role in my life later on, was sent off in the first transport. He was just sixteen. His parents tore their hair out over his departure. He was an only child, pampered by his mother, grandmother and father alike. He had always had everything he wanted and showed little appreciation for it.

Everyone thought on the quiet that he would come to no good, but fate plays strange tricks with people. Overnight he turned into a warrior: strong, brave and fearless. His parents thought they would never see him again. But they did, albeit briefly, ten months later, when they were reunited in Terezín.

The whispers and rumours had suddenly proved true and turned into reality before our eyes. Gradually we accepted the fact that there was no escape from the Germans and their plans for us, and we had to resign ourselves to everything that lay in store. Our prayers, Arno's and mine, were simply that we should not be sent on separate transports. If God loved us he must let us go together, indivisibly, wherever we were to be sent. As long as we stayed together, nothing bad could happen to us.

20

Our departure

Well, our turn did come, sooner than we had expected. At the beginning of January 1942, we were summoned to a large nearby town to be registered. This took place in the main hall of some district office. There was a great crowd assembled from the whole area – people from towns, villages and isolated communities. We stood in rows facing the uniformed Germans behind the table. Each of us stepped forward, gave his name and address and was given a narrow slip of paper with a transport number.

My heart was beating with fear, not about where I would be sent, but lest Arno should be sent somewhere different. He and his family were in the row in front of me and already had their registration slips. Their transport had the letter R. I was trembling to know what mine would be. It was like a roulette game. Nobody had the faintest idea what would turn up.

We were out of luck. My family and I were assigned to transport S. My worst fears had been realised; Arno and I would be separated. In my despair I felt like falling on my knees and imploring the SS man to let us go together. But I knew that any pleading would be worse than useless. The crowd was tense and noisy and the Germans started shouting: *"Aufgehen! Aufgehen!"* – "Keep Moving!" – to try and speed things up. "Let's be finished with you!" Blows fell even at this stage.

Suddenly I noticed amid the confusion that my mother, who was the first of us to be called, had S 204 on her slip, my brother S 205, my sister S 206. Mine was S 716! I felt as if some icy hand of destiny had touched me. What could this mean? I would be leaving in the same transport, but at some point fate would separate us. Was this a good or a bad sign? In my misery I decided it must be bad. I was full of apprehension. In that room, in the space of a few hours, they had transformed us into numbers and played havoc with our lives. I who had been determined to go to the end of the world, to the very depths of hell with Arno, was now here on my own, cut off from him and from my own family too.

Transport R was to leave on 16 January 1942, destination unknown. The Germans never revealed things in advance. Perhaps it was bound for Terezín, perhaps for elsewhere. I was distraught. Arno was leaving me. Why did our love have to be so brief? Perhaps God in heaven would take pity on us and send us to the same place. I grasped at the faintest hope and persuaded myself that all was not yet lost. I sat with his family until they were taken away, helping to roll up Arno's socks to put in his case. I took the chain and four-leafed clover charm that I wore around my neck and put it in his hand:

"There, take that for luck."

Next morning they were on their way.

Our S transport was due to go four days later, on 20 January. There was no time for lamentation now. We were leaving home and we had to get everything ready. Each person was allowed to take one suitcase and a bedroll: a pillow, a sheet and if possible a blanket. All this was rolled up in a canvas bag with the transport number sewn onto it. The suitcase also had to be carefully labelled, with the transport number painted indelibly in large white letters across the front.

The next question was what to put in the case. Clothes? Food? For how long? Winter things? Summer things? Everyone's advice was different. One well-meaning neighbour slipped through our door and counselled us earnestly: "The most important thing to take is boots. Warm, comfortable ones. Supposing you have to march somewhere? Then warm underclothing. And gloves. Woolly caps. Hands, feet and head have to be kept warm."

Someone else said it was more important to take food: bread, tins of fat drippings, and so forth. Our former shop assistant Matýsek (as Father called him after his fifteen years' service) also came to tell us what he had learned from the grapevine: "Forget about food and clothing. What you must have is a supply of soap and, above all, cigarettes. Cigarettes are the most valuable currency in those places, I'm told. You can get whatever you want with them. I have this from someone who knows the local police on duty around Terezín. They can't be wrong." And he stuck to this advice.

In fact, he was quite right. Cigarettes were indeed the top currency. Soap was already rationed and hard to come by. In any case, it was poor, sandy stuff, and was always in short supply.

We packed a bit of everything in our cases. Warm clothing, a few tins of food, soap cubes and, if there was still room, a supply of that highly rated wartime exchange commodity, cigarettes.

Finally we tidied up the house meticulously, leaving everything shipshape as if we were going off on a summer holiday and wanted things to be orderly when we got back.

I sat down at the piano for the last time and played two pieces that seemed to convey a sense of hope: Dvorák's Waltz in D flat major and Sinding's "Rustle of Spring." Then I stroked the keys goodbye and closed the lid. I even locked it so that nothing untoward should happen to it before we met again.

21

Terezín camp

Early next morning we got ready to leave. It was Tuesday, 20 January 1942, a beautiful winter day with a cloudless sky. The temperature was well below freezing, there was frost on the trees, and the cold stung your nose – the sort of day that, at other times, made you glad to be alive. We loaded our cases and other baggage onto a two-wheeled pushcart and set off for the railway station. My brother and I pulled the cart while my mother and sister walked behind it with heads bowed liked bereaved relatives at a funeral. People who met us either looked away or slipped quickly into doorways to hide their true thoughts. Did they feel sympathy, or loathing? A few actually shouted words of encouragement, like, "Don't worry! You'll soon be back."

Others came up to us quietly, muttering, "It's your turn now. It'll be ours next."

On the way, I ran into my best friend, Vera. She was wearing woollen stockings, a bright warm sweater, red knitted cap and gloves to match. She was carrying her tie-on skates in one hand and the fastening key in the other. She stopped.

"Where are you off to?" she asked.

"Don't really know. They haven't told us. Some concentration camp, I expect."

"Ah, that's silly. There was a deep frost overnight. Down to minus fifteen, I think. The ice'll be strong today. Pity you can't come. Perhaps you'll be back before the winter's over. The water's sure to stay frozen for a long time. Cheerio, then!"

"Cheerio!"

So Vera went off to skate, and I went ... who could say where?

In the big town nearby a train was standing ready on a siding, with a huge crowd of people milling around it: young, old, mothers with children. All around them on the ground lay their luggage with the white names and transport numbers. The whole group was surrounded by uniformed SS men. Some of them were holding dogs on the leash, others were going around shouting orders and pushing people in.

"*Alle einsteigen!*" "Everyone get in! Right away – faster, faster!"

Everything was in confusion. Children were screaming and mothers were trying to quieten them, though they were just as scared themselves. Some people were too old to climb in quickly and blows rained down.

Father's words rang in my ears: "Just keep calm. Remember, calmness is strength."

I wondered where he was now. The thought struck me that even if he could write a letter we would never get it. And he would never find out where we went.

It was everyone for himself now – to the best of his ability.

And what about Arno? How would it all end? Would we ever see each other again? Life had suddenly become one huge question-mark.

———————✦———————

Crammed full of people and luggage, the train finally moved off. Before it did so, every compartment was securely locked and brown-uniformed *Schutzpolizei*, police guards, all drunk, were ordered to keep watch over us. They carried short whips, with lead balls on the end and patrolled the whole train continuously, from coach to coach. There were a lot of them. As soon as they came into a coach they yelled out "*Achtung!*" and everyone had to get up and stand at attention. If anyone was asleep he was whipped across the face. Woe to anyone who was not clean-shaven. They would shave his beard off with a dry razor until the skin bled. If there was no blood, there was no fun in it for them. I gradually grew accustomed, though never reconciled, to German brutality and sadism.

Outside the train windows the same gently rolling landscape flashed by: familiar fields with a crow pecking in a furrow here and there, the silent trees alongside the snow-covered tracks – the same scene as when we rode along that very stretch to visit Grandmother in Prague. How I had always enjoyed watching at the window and looking forward to getting off at the Wilson Central Station where everyone would welcome us.

Now here we were, prisoners in locked coaches. This time it was the landscape outside, silent and sad, looking in at us.

———————✦———————

Our train stopped on sidings from time to time. It took two days and two nights for us to reach our destination, Terezín. I was impatient to get out. For me, Terezín meant a possible reunion with Arno, who I hoped was as eager to see me as I him. Any moment now our eyes would meet and we would fall into each other's arms. Just be patient. Terezín was the answer to my prayers, the place where I most yearned to go. God had been kind to us after all.

Arno was the centre of my life. All I longed for was to be with him again. Hunger, cold, discomfort and fear of the Germans – these held no terror for me. Nothing mattered more than being with Arno again, firmly hand in hand.

Etched in front of our eyes at last were the walls of Terezín. In the middle of the city gate was the green uniform of a Czech gendarme. We did not have to worry about finding ourselves in some unknown place in a foreign country. We were still on the territory of our Czechoslovak Republic and that was some comfort. The gendarmes were speaking Czech, which seemed a good sign. They escorted us through the inner town, its square street grid lined with low houses on either side.

The dominant feature, however, was a group of about ten huge barracks, three or four storeys high, enclosing large courtyards. At each level, on all four sides of the courtyard, there was a long gallery from corner to corner. Until now Terezín had been a town where garrisons were quartered in the barracks and civilians lived in the houses. Just before our arrival the army had been moved out, but the civilian population of about 5,000 remained.

Each barracks had a German name, of some German city or region. Thus there was now a Dresden barracks (Dresden for short), Hamburg, Magdeburg, Hannover, Sudetenkaserne, Hohenelbe (Vrchlabí for us Czechs), Kavalier (Kavalírka), and so on.

Each building acquired a new character according to its

inmates. Sudeten and Hannover were men's quarters. Dresden and Hamburg were for women only. Magdeburg became the centre of activities. It housed the Terezín administrative centre and the Jewish Council of Elders. In a building on the town square was the German *Kommandantura*, the German High Command Headquarters.

Our transport was quickly split up into men and women with children.

All the men were allocated to Sudeten while we women went to Hamburg. Our family was now split; my brother went off with the other men and we three women prepared to move into the women's quarters. For the moment, we stood with our baggage on the courtyard waiting to have rooms, or billets, assigned to us. These billets were entered from the long galleries around the courtyards. Each contained three-tier bunks put up by the boys from the first *Arbeitskommando*. The bunks were designed according to our new living space allowance – about eight square metres per person. Bunks were separated by narrow corridors. Each little billet was equipped with at least four or five bunks, thus accommodating twelve to fifteen people.

We were prepared for what the Germans in the train had promised us – to sleep on concrete or outside in the frost – but instead we had own bed in a room with a roof overhead, sheltered from rain and wind, where you could stretch out and sleep under your own blanket. It seemed luxury indeed, even if your living space was only twenty-seven square feet.

Our billet was on the third floor and we were lucky to be given a bunk by the window. We divided our family premises up so that Mother was sleeping on the bottom tier, my sister in the middle and I on the top with a small ladder attached to it. We stuffed the cases under Mother's bed, fixed some coat-hooks to the wall, and laid out our utensils and dishes on the window sill. And there we were, settled in our new "flat."

As per instructions we elected a *Zimmerälteste* or "room leader", who had to see not only that the billet was tidy but that peace and quiet prevailed among its inmates. Her most important job was to divide up the bread ration twice a week. As long as we still had supplies of food brought from home, we were very happy to get our third of a loaf each time. But once they ran out we eyed each portion most critically in terms of size and fair share.

We had to accustom ourselves very quickly to living in such close quarters – one room – with other people. We were all in the same situation but everyone reacted differently. Older women became depressed and intolerant, and complained about things incessantly. We younger ones took it in a more sporting spirit, as if we were sleeping under canvas in a girl scouts' summer camp. But we all suddenly found ourselves thrown together with new people we had never met, and began to form new friendships.

22

Love in a cellar

My main concern was when and where to meet Arno. Each barracks with its new quota of civilians was sealed off and no one could get out. Although I had found out that Arno was quartered in a building just around the corner, he was as far away from me as if he were living on another planet. I started to fret. I had been here a week and still there was no contact. Supposing they sent him off somewhere else, "further east", as the phrase went, and we never saw each other again? Life began to seem absurd. Yet the thought that he was living, breathing and sleeping only a short distance away, and thinking about me as I was about him, warmed my heart. I was sure he would find some opportunity to get out of his barracks. I didn't have to wait long.

The rumour spread through our galleries one day that a new supply of potatoes had reached the barracks, destined for the communal kitchen. As I ran out of our billet I could hear our signature tune being whistled, loud and clear.

It had to be Arno! I ran over to the low gallery wall with such a rush that I almost toppled down into the courtyard from the third floor. There he was, as large as life, standing with six other men next to a cartload of potatoes. He had his belted winter coat on and was looking around to find me. I ran down the staircase as if it were a playground slide and our eyes met immediately.

Meanwhile, someone was organising a squad of twenty women to peel potatoes. I immediately volunteered and was luckily included. The rest had to go back into their billets. Arno was standing among the men unloading the potatoes. Only a few metres separated us. We were longing frantically to fall into each other's arms. But how? And where?

Amidst the sudden commotion in the yard we managed to get away from the others and ran into the corridor, where there were stairs leading down. We followed these and found ourselves in a cellar which had storage rooms. Each room had a heavy iron door. We had but little time, and the desire was great.

Throwing ourselves at the first door, we found it locked tight. The same with the door next to it. Desperately we pushed at a third door, blinded by ardour and oblivious to the danger. The door gave way, creaking just a little.

Huddled into a dark corner by the door we kissed with insane passion – and all the rest. The barracks seemed to vanish, along with the Germans, Terezín and time itself. There was nothing but us, and this moment. Here, together, one soul, one body alone in the universe. I cannot say how long this trip outside reality lasted.

Suddenly we heard footsteps in the corridor outside: heavy, regular, military ones. No question about it, a German patrol. By the sound, there must be three of them, and now we could hear their voices too. We now knew that the game was up. They would be bound to find us, and the penalty was death. I could only pray that we would not be tortured as well.

They unlocked the first door and looked inside. Then the second one next to ours. We stood pressed to the wall, clinched together. If they were going to check every cellar methodically, ours would be the next. They stopped in front of our door, pressed the handle down, and evidently wondered why the door was not locked like the others.

"*Was ist da los?*" "What's up with this one?"

One of the Germans pushed it open with a jerk. The door banged against the wall, creating a little corner in which we stood close together. One SS man came and planted himself in the doorway. I, pressed against the wall, could see the soles of his boots. We held our breath. Only the thickness of the door panel stood between us and certain death.

"*Mach doch mal Licht!*" the commander ordered. "Let's have some light!"

Our hearts stopped as they switched on powerful torches that lit up the whole cellar. For an eternity the cone of brightness travelled over the walls and the floor. The dust started to irritate my nose and I wanted to sneeze. God help me, please – that would be our death sentence. With an enormous effort of will I managed to avert certain catastrophe.

"*Weiter gehen!*" "Next!"

The order to proceed rang out. Finding nothing, they switched their torches off and left, banging the cellar door behind them.

Supposing they locked us in now? What would become of us? But they didn't.

It was some time before we came to our senses again. As soon as the sound of their footsteps had died away we ran upstairs into the courtyard, where the potatoes had all been unloaded. I quickly resumed my place among the potato peelers while Arno joined his own squad, which was just leaving. We exchanged a quick look in silent farewell.

We knew it would be a while before we saw one another again, but the memory of this encounter would keep our hearts warm.

———❉———

Meanwhile more and more transports from Prague and other Czech cities kept pouring into Terezín. Among the newcomers were friends and relatives whom we had been prevented from visiting by the new race laws. And now, here we were, all together. Even Grandmother turned up. We managed to get her into our billet. With the help of cigarettes we changed bunks so that she could move right next to us in our corner. Mother was so happy to have her near and did all she could to look after her.

Terezín now filled up so rapidly that the 5,000 original inhabitants had to be moved out at short notice. It really looked as if it were meant as a permanent colony for all the Jews of Bohemia and Moravia. There was even a slight relaxation of the rules on movement between male and female barracks and it became possible to get an exit permit on various grounds.

Arno always managed to find a pretext. His so-called "forwarding detachment" had more freedom of movement than anyone. It was they who brought in food supplies and took them from barracks to barracks, so he often turned up at Hamburg. He only had to whistle and we had a chance to see each other and exchange news, however briefly. I had a permanent place with the potato squad. The peelings were carted off to German farmers in the surrounding countryside, who fed them to their pigs. But I always managed to sneak a few into our billet for Mother to make hot soup on a little stove.

The bodies in our overcrowded rooms and bunks attracted fleas and bedbugs.

These multiplied fast and crawled up the walls, where they were swatted and left red stains behind. When we ate they would sometimes fall into a plate of soup. We scooped them out gingerly on the tip of a spoon, so as to waste as little soup as possible, flicked them onto the floor, squashed them and carried on eating.

One day in March, Arno unexpectedly appeared with a birthday present for me: a little folding stool made out of bits of wood he had picked up somewhere. We fitted this into our family corner and now we could say we had some furniture. Anyone could sit on it who wanted to, but it was I who had the most enjoyment from it and carved his name on it.

As winter slowly gave way to spring, hopes rose that we might be home again for the summer. But the reality was very different. Not only did more and more transports arrive, but more and more left as well.

Where to, was a secret. "To the East," was all we were told. So everyone dreaded them, though no one knew what awaited them at the other end. No one had been known to return, no reports ever reached us. The very word "east" acquired sinister undertones. There was no predictable pattern. One day there would be a transport composed of whole families. Another would consist only of people over sixty-five, or only of young men fit for hard labour. No one had any reliable information. It was all fear and speculation. But as long as we remained in Terezín we seemed to enjoy relative safety. We felt almost at home.

The central registration office in Magdeburg, where the Jewish self-administration Council of Elders operated, worked in shirts around the clock. As people arrived and left, every name had to be recorded, along with the person's age and transport number. If you were unlucky you got a narrow pink slip with your name and transport number on it, and had to present yourself within twenty-four hours at the train standing on the siding. There you got into a cattle truck which the Germans locked and sealed, and the train moved off into the unknown with its human cargo.

This was the fate that befell Arno and his family one day in June 1942. He came to tell me outside the hours his job permitted, flouting the risk of being caught. He felt he had nothing more to lose now. All he could say was, "We've been put on a penal transport. It's a reprisal for the killing of Heydrich." We all knew the senior German official in Prague, *Reichsprotektor* Reinhard Heydrich, had been assassinated.

I was dumbstruck.

His transport of two thousand people was to leave the following day. I woke at four that morning. Arno was standing on a pair of steps over my bunk, wearing his grey belted coat and all ready to go. I have no idea how he had managed to get into our barracks at that time of night. He was breathless with excitement. He took my hand, slipped a little tin ring over my finger and said, "That's for our engagement. And to keep you safe. If we're both alive when the war ends, I'll find you."

He embraced me and kissed me, and jumped down. Closing the door quietly behind him, he was gone. At five o'clock he left with the rest of his transport.

On the inside of his homemade tin ring he had engraved *Arno 13.6.1942.*

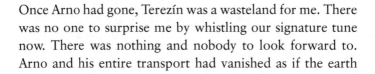

Once Arno had gone, Terezín was a wasteland for me. There was no one to surprise me by whistling our signature tune now. There was nothing and nobody to look forward to. Arno and his entire transport had vanished as if the earth had swallowed them up. There were no rumours, even, as to where they might have been taken. Not the slightest scrap of information. What was the difference between an everyday transport "to the East" and a "penal transport"? No one knew the answer.

I felt sure that with all his courage and resourcefulness Arno would manage to adapt and find the strength to survive all the hardships and cruelty that lay in wait. The war was sure to end soon and then we would somehow find each other. I had his ring on my finger and this would bind us together, whatever the distance that separated us.

There was no time for tears and personal woes now. It was a collective tragedy that had descended on us all, like some natural disaster that forces people together. All that remained was hope and the determination to survive. People continued to say goodbye to each other, wish each other a safe journey and a happy return. We all trusted that this storm of rage and madness would one day blow over, that we would all come together again, return to our homes and start new lives.

———✦———

Spring was well on its way now, but none of us had yet returned home as our neighbours had been predicting when we left. It occurred to me that the ice on the skating pond must long since have melted and Vera put her skates away in the cupboard for next winter. There would be willows and lamb's tails in the bushes all around. Would I ever see them again? We lived in a different world these days, where nothing grew and nothing blossomed. There was no green grass, just the massive, cheerless barracks walls. The memory of our moment of love, Arno's and mine, in that storage room soon after we arrived was all that kept my heart warm.

23

Life in Terezín

The evacuation of the previous Terezín inhabitants had to be speeded up as fresh transports of thousands of people flooded in – now not only from Bohemia, but from German cities such as Aachen, Cologne and Berlin. The new arrivals from Germany were mainly elderly people with masses of luggage. They had been told they were being taken to spas where they would lack for nothing, medically or socially, so many of them had packed dinner suits and evening dresses with the long gloves and feather hats that were then in fashion.

On arrival, their luggage was loaded onto black, long-shafted funeral carts with fancy carving. Under normal circumstances they would have been pulled by horses, but at Terezín they were pulled by ten boys from the forwarding detachment. These four-wheeled carts were the only means of conveyance available in the town, and were used for transporting all manner of things: cases, loaves from the baker, groceries, and sometimes people from the incoming transports who were too old to walk. On other occasions they served their traditional purpose and took corpses to the crematorium. Terezín wasn't an extermination camp, but with disease, malnutrition and so many elderly, the crematorium was kept busy.

Transports came, transports went; no sooner had people exchanged welcome greetings than they were parting again, saying goodbye. Everywhere it was as busy as could be and the town never paused for breath. On the contrary, once the 5,000 original inhabitants had been moved out, new ones came in until the population totalled nearly 60,000.

Every free space had to be utilised for living quarters. Not only the barracks but all the surrounding houses and even shop windows were used for accommodation, with three-tier bunks installed everywhere for living and sleeping. All the barracks gates were opened now and we were able to move freely about the town and visit each other. It really seemed as if things were looking up.

Only Arno was missing. How happy we would have been here now.

One day a Prague transport arrived with the parents and grandmother of Bedrich, the one who had bewitched me with *You are my lucky star*. When sixteen-year-old Bedrich had been taken off in the very first transport to Terezín, his parents had never thought they would see him again. And yet they did, in this very spot. There was joy and there were tears of happiness. They had brought supplies of fresh food with them. We had a great party, just as we used to have in their Prague home, and celebrated our lucky reunion. Life seemed not so terrible after all. But the gaiety was short lived. Just ten days elapsed before Bedrich's father, mother and grandmother were summoned to join the next transport to the East. All the joy of reunion was replaced with partings, sadness and tears.

For the time being Bedrich himself stayed on with us. Apparently the authorities were not including healthy young men in the transports, as these were needed at the moment to keep the town and all its services functioning. Every able-bodied person was now mobilised. Terezín was turned into a little autonomous state of its own, run by the Council of Elders with its own triumvirate.

This comprised three academics from three different universities: Prague, Berlin and Vienna. They all had similar names: Dr Edelstein, Dr Epstein and Dr Murmelstein. This strange trio was picked by the Germans to secure the smooth and efficient running of all communal affairs, but also to decide the composition of transports to the East, a thousand people at a time – against their will, against their conscience.

We scarcely saw any Germans on the streets. They all sat in their large building, the *Kommandantura*, the headquarters from where they issued orders, punished offences and dispatched people on their way – to somewhere.

We never knew what happened to them afterwards.

24

The kitchen

To feed 60,000 people three times a day, however inadequately, was no small task. Huge kitchens were set up in the cellars of all the big barracks, each to cook for 6,000.

I was now promoted from potato peeling to kitchen duty in Hannover. It looked less like a kitchen than a major industrial production unit. Great 50-litre cauldrons were installed close together along three sides of the area and heated from underneath. To be a kitchen stoker was a superior and much sought-after job.

In front of each cauldron was a wooden step on which we stood to stir whatever was cooking inside. There were no choice ingredients. Morning and evening we made "coffee," a warm brown concoction of coffee substitute. At noon there was "food". Once or twice a week this featured meat – that is, a slice of horsemeat with a little brown cube of gravy, plus one potato. Sometimes the same meat was served as "goulash."

Once a week there was a yeast dumpling with "chocolate" sauce, a brown liquid made from some other synthetic powder with artificial sweetener. Sometimes there was just a watery soup with a slice of parsnip and a piece of potato floating in it. In the evening there was "coffee" again.

We worked around the clock in three shifts. The first shift was from 2 a.m. to 10 a.m.; the second from 10 a.m. to 6 p.m.; and the third from 6 p.m. to 2 a.m. again. Each group consisted of fifteen to twenty people – men and women mixed – under a leader, the *parták*, as we Czech-speakers called him. We were issued with rubber boots because the concrete floor was always wet, having to be continually swept and hosed down. Cleanliness had to be maintained, but there was no avoiding untoward incidents. There were pipes running along the walls, as is usual in basements. On one night shift when "goulash" was being cooked, a large grey rat was seen scurrying along the pipe. There was a great commotion. The girls screamed, but the boys were merciless. The rat stopped to look around. One of the boys egged on his friend next to him, "Why don't you take that shovel, Otouš, and knock him off into the cauldron!"

Without much hesitation Otouš swung the shovel around and felled the animal into the goulash. Everyone was delighted, "We got it!"

When the *parták* saw what had happened he bellowed, "Fish it out right away and don't breathe a word to anybody!"

Otouš, however, feeling he deserved credit for successfully disposing of the rat, wouldn't have it. "Oh, why not leave it in? At least there will be more meat."

One WIPO guard (short for *Wirtschaftspolizei* or "household police") was allocated to each kitchen to ensure that no food was stolen. Rations reached the kitchen in quantities precisely calculated on a scale fixed by the Germans. The WIPO were the inmates' own inspectorate and were responsible for any losses or thefts, for which there were severe penalties. But we all behaved impeccably and everything went as it should.

There was an 8 o'clock curfew in the town which had to be strictly observed. Anyone caught on the street after that time was punished. Only those who needed to move about in the town after hours to perform their various duties had official passes. All of us who worked on the night shift in the kitchens had these passes in case we were stopped by a patrol.

The streets at night were not only empty but unlit, and there was total darkness. I always carried in my pocket, along with my pass, a Dynamo flashlight. This was a great treasure of mine. I had brought it with me from home and in these days I really needed it. It looked like a little grey mouse and fitted neatly into my palm. It recharged automatically if you rhythmically squeezed a little metal lever. As I went along it kept on whistling to itself – *ooh-eee, ooh-eee* – so one had the feeling of not being alone.

Walking around Terezín at night, you might think you were in a haven of peace and safety. Not a sound, not a sign of life. You couldn't tell there were 60,000 weary, hungry souls here, spending restless nights in their eight square metres of living space, awaiting their fate.

No cat or dog ever ran across the street.

Food was distributed regularly three times a day. A large container of soup, for example, would be placed in a recess in the kitchen, filled with an exact number of helpings. We stood behind the soup with a ladle in hand. In front of this recess stood a duty officer of the *Menage-dienst*, a ticket controller, equipped with a little punch for making a hole in the meal coupon that everyone had to produce when they went for their food. It was like having your ticket punched by a train conductor.

Long before any food appeared in the recess there was a long, long line of people waiting patiently with their mess tins and spoons ready. The majority were old people who stood still, huddled together, silent and hungry. One could see from their expressions that the one ladle of soup meant the chance of surviving perhaps one more day. It was a sad job serving them. An old man would come up, hold out his tin with trembling hand and mutter imploringly: "*Von unten, bitte, Fräulein.*" "From the bottom, miss, please." There was always the hope that a ladle scraping the bottom might bring up a piece of potato or cabbage that would make their day, as if they had won a small lottery prize. We always tried to be helpful.

Of those sick or elderly men and women condemned to spend the rest of their days here, about two hundred died every day. And more and more of them were now arriving, through an endless revolving door. Off the transports and into Terezín, then back onto the transports for the journey east.

One day Marta, my friend from the English Institute, turned up on a Prague transport.

We fell around each other's necks like long-lost sisters. Marta had married Karel Bloch, a wonderful doctor who sadly suffered from tuberculosis. She was quick to introduce me to her husband, a haggard man with twinkling eyes. There was no tragedy in his appearance, and Marta was obviously happy.

They were both immediately assigned to the medical staff: Karel as a doctor and Marta as a nurse, both entitled to wear a uniform. They were not billeted together, but we all often met when our shifts allowed, sitting in her room or on my bunk, and chatting endlessly. It was lovely to be together. We did not miss the ambience of a smart café or a posh flat with soft armchairs. We were simply together, that was the main thing.

It was around this time that the Accommodation Department started allocating small spaces on the extensive attic floors to some of the more distinguished inmates to create "penthouses" for themselves. A penthouse was meant for married couples and there were many applicants for the privilege. The lucky ones either had contacts in high places or simply paid for their penthouse as on any black market.

Soon after the penthouses started proliferating in all the buildings, dormer windows with curtains began to appear on every roof. Some people seemed to be settling down, as if they expected to stay there for good.

Here and there the end section of a long corridor was fenced off with a wooden partition, giving rise to a *kumbál*, a cubby-hole just for one person. I tried applying for one of these on the grounds of irregular working hours and the impossibility of sleeping during the day in the billet with so many people around. I had a few good friends in high places. They helped me to get my cubby-hole at the end of a long corridor, with a window, in one of the former private houses. My friends in the carpentry shop made me a wooden partition, a door with a lock, a few shelves on the wall, a folding table, and a cupboard in the corner for my coat and clothes, over which I hung a green-coloured sheet. They fixed up a bedstead and mattress, and there was a little stove under the window to heat the place in the winter. My new room was reminiscent of a sleeping compartment in a night train – an absolute luxury for one person.

Just opposite me in another cubby-hole lived a well-known Prague nightclub musician, Wolfi Lederer, and his wife. I had good neighbours.

But I had scarcely had time to settle in when I suddenly found myself in mortal danger.

25

Marta and her nurse's uniform

One day news got around that a transport was leaving for the East in two days time, composed entirely of sick and old people.

Nobody I knew was on the list, so I went on calmly with my work. The following evening at about ten o'clock I saw from my window two boys with a stretcher coming into my building. I assumed they were picking up one of those elderly persons destined for the transport, and settled back in bed with a book.

A moment later came a knock on my own door. I opened up and there were the two young men with the stretcher. They must have failed to find the person they're looking for, I thought, and have come to ask where she lives. Not a bit of it. They had a slip with my name on it: Fantlová Zdenka.

"Is this you?" they asked.

The situation struck me as ridiculous. "Yes, that's my name," I said dismissively, "but there must be some mistake. After all, as you can see, I'm neither ill nor elderly."

They took another look at the slip. "This is your name, clear enough, so we'll have to follow orders and take you along to the Podmokly sluice." This was the collecting point for those about to be transported.

In moments like these one's brains work fast. If they

carry me off on this stretcher I'm done for, I thought. I mustn't on any account leave this room. It struck me that I had a good friend, Pavel, who was on duty that night at the central register in the administrative building and must know what had happened. He would have to help in some way to get me off this transport list.

There was no time to lose. The young porters were standing over me with their stretcher propped against the wall. I grabbed pencil and paper and wrote: "My name's on the transport list and they've come to take me to the sluice. Tell me quickly what to do." I folded the paper, wrote Pavel's name on it, and gave one of the lads one of my three last cigarettes to take it to Magdeburg, find Pavel and come back with an answer. He took a little while. All kinds of thoughts were racing through my head.

Surely, I said to myself, I can't just go off on my own with no warning to anyone. Not even my mother would know that I had suddenly disappeared. That can't be possible, I argued. But in my heart I knew that anything was possible here. Half an hour later the young man returned with the answer. But it was not what I had expected.

"Let them carry you away. Leave the rest to me."

There was nothing else for me to do. I felt sure I would be back very soon and had no need to dress for anything. So they carted me off just as I was, in my nightdress with a blanket thrown over me. It was about eleven o'clock when we arrived at the Podmokly barracks. This was on the edge of the town and behind it was the siding where the transport train stood ready.

We went down a long drive lined with uniformed SS men on either side, checking the new arrivals. One of them had a list from which he crossed off the name of each stretcher case. The reception panel included two Jewish doctors, officially nominated. The situation looked bad.

I knew full well that no one who entered the collecting centre ever got out. If anyone tried to escape from a transport he was sure to be caught and end up in the *Kleine Festung*, the Little Fortress in the Terezín tower, to be shot or hanged. Several people had already met their end there.

The porters carried me on up a wooden staircase to the first floor, where the collecting centre was. It was a huge bare room full of people lying on stretchers, one beside another. I shut my eyes.

An official kept shouting out names and whoever answered was quickly carried away. After about half an hour I heard my name called:

"Fantlová Zdenka!"

I kept mum – not a word – and kept my eyes shut. I mustn't answer at any price. Perhaps there was still a chance that my friend could work some miracle to save me.

Time passed. They kept bringing in more and more people. But a great number had also been taken away.

"Fantlová Zdenka!"

Again I heard my name being read out. My heart was throbbing. Supposing Pavel, with the best will in the world, had not managed to get me off the list? I would be taken away with all these sick old people in just my nightdress and one blanket – to goodness knows where!

I began to be really scared. The clock on the wall said 2 a.m.

At this moment Pavel came into the room, and my eyes lit up at the sight of this angel arriving to save me. But he hadn't.

"Zdenka," he said miserably, "it looks bad. There's no chance of getting you off the list at this point. But perhaps something can be done. Dr Pepík Skalský will be coming along in a moment and may be able to dream something up.

Meanwhile, don't answer at all if they call your name."

I started to realise how grim the situation was.

Dr Pepík Skalský was a fair-haired young man of farming stock from our own part of the country. He had been a good friend of my brother's. I waited impatiently for him, as the ranks of stretcher cases began to thin out.

"Fantlová Zdenka!" The official was calling out my name at shorter intervals now. As long as I stay silent I've got a chance, I told myself, and kept my eyes fixed on the door. Suddenly I saw Pepík coming in. I motioned to show him where I was. He knelt down next to me and said very seriously, "The only way to get you off the transport now is if I give you an injection of milk. You'll get a high temperature and they don't take people with fever. Don't answer to your name yet. I'll come back in a moment with everything necessary." He hurried out.

"Fantlová Zdenka!" There was my name again. The official looked all around the now half-empty room. Time dragged on inexorably. I must not, must not answer. No one here knows who I am, and even if I have to go, I must be the last one.

After half an hour Pepík was back again. Being a doctor he could come and go as he pleased. And amid all the uncertainties of Terezín there was one thing we could be sure of: we always helped one another to the best of our abilities, even in the dead of night. Everyone did his best for a friend.

He squatted down beside me with his little case and the injection he had prepared. But I now felt entirely at the mercy of fate, and had decided on a different course.

In a calm voice that surprised even me, I told him my thoughts.

"Look, it is very kind of you to be willing to give me this injection. But I can see they're sending people off when they're not fit for transport – even fever cases. You know what I think? If I am destined to go off into the unknown with this transport, I'd sooner go well and strong, rather than ill. I shall have a better chance at the end of the journey, or wherever we go after that, if I'm healthy. So thanks for everything. You did what you could."

Pepík was speechless, partly in sudden despair over what was going to happen to me, but partly because he felt I was probably right. He sat by me for a moment longer. "Whatever you think. I won't force you. When it comes to a decisive point, everyone knows best where his own strength lies."

"Fantlová Zdenka!" We both heard it this time. No fresh cases were being brought in. Suddenly I had a brainstorm. It was as if some unknown power had surged up inside me and was telling me what to do – some last-minute instinct of self-preservation.

"Pepík," I burst out. "I have an idea. Marta, she's the only one who can help me now. Go to the Dresden barracks quickly and find her. She isn't on duty tonight. Ask her to come here right away and bring a nurse's uniform with her, wrapped up. Please, Pepík, hurry. We have very little time."

He agreed and ran out through the door.

The clock now showed 3.45 a.m. *They'll take me, they'll take me not. They'll take me, they'll take me not*, the clock hands seemed to chant softly.

"Fantlová Zdenka!" echoed hollowly through the half-empty hall. My life was really on the cliff edge now, and my heart was beating so loudly I was afraid the official might hear it. Time was running out. If Marta failed to come, I was doomed.

At that moment she appeared in the doorway like a *deus ex machina*. Wearing her nurse's uniform, she came straight towards me. There was no time for friendly exchanges.

"Help me to the loo," I said. "It's at the end of the corridor."

Supporting me like a sick patient, she slowly led me along. We both walked into the cubicle and bolted the door. At lightning speed I put on the spare uniform over my nightdress. I had left the blanket on the stretcher. We decided to walk straight out of the barracks together, like two nurses on duty. Fortune favours the brave and the daring.

We ran downstairs to the corridor where there were still a few SS men standing. Arm in arm, we exchanged lively talk and even laughed a little to show how casually we were going off duty. I shivered inwardly, but we passed them calmly enough and went out through the barracks gate onto the street. We had won. The miracle had happened. I was free for the moment. But what next? We had to stop after the next corner and try to calm ourselves down.

It was not all over yet, however. The total size of the transport had to tally exactly with the names and numbers on the list, and everything was rigorously checked. The death penalty for attempted escape from a transport applied equally to failure to report. My name had not yet been taken off the list. Marta came to a decision. One of the doctors on duty there was a close friend of her husband, Karel.

"Wait here for me," she said. "I will go back there and explain that I have to speak to him urgently."

As a nurse she could re-enter the barracks freely. She found a chance to have a quick word with the doctor, who promised her he would get my name taken off, which he managed to do at his own risk.

I vanished from the list, and from the transport.

At 5 a.m., with all the coaches locked, the train pulled away. It was not until after the war that we found out where it had gone. It went to Auschwitz, and all its passengers, without exception, were taken straight to the gas chambers.

26

The woods of Křivoklát

Christmas and New Year slipped across the calendar and sank like the sun below the horizon. We had been in Terezín for a year now. Apart from Father, we were all still together: my grandmother, mother, brother, sister and myself. Gradually we were forgetting our old home. Life was quite different here. There were lots of us, all supporting one another in the hope and longing that we could survive and hold out in this place until the end of the war. We all tried to live normally, however abnormal the conditions.

There was no shortage of fresh developments, and new regulations were announced every day. No one ever expected them to bring good tidings. However, one day a piece of news ran around the town which for a while lit up the surrounding gloom like a brief flash of sun breaking merrily through a grey pall of clouds.

ONE THOUSAND YOUNG WOMEN ARE TO VOLUNTEER TOMORROW FOR TREE PLANTING IN THE KŘIVOKLÁT WOODS. FOR ONE MONTH. DEPARTURE IN TWO DAYS TIME.

I jumped for joy and decided to enrol immediately. An excursion from Terezín to the Bohemian forest sounded like a month's holiday in complete liberty. My decision, and my evident delight, nearly made Mother collapse.

"You must be crazy! At a time and place like this no one rushes into anything voluntarily. How do you know where they'll take you off to? They may promise you all sorts of things, but you can't trust a German. You stay put. I forbid you to go."

But the passage of time had changed the rules of our game. We weren't at home any more, where Mother could exercise her authority. That had gone by the wayside. Now I was twenty and making vital decisions for myself. Still, I tried to reassure her.

"Don't worry, they obviously need us very badly for this tree planting. You'll see. Everything will turn out all right and I shall be back in a month's time."

I couldn't wait to see the green trees and smell their aroma. I signed up and in two days was off with the entire group by train to Křivoklát, exactly as they promised.

They split us up into groups of fifty girls. My group was housed in a big log cabin deep in the forest. In front of it was a little hut for two gendarmes who were there to guard us. They were middle-aged men, quite friendly and jolly, it seemed to me. They even smiled at us. We all talked Czech together and felt as if we were on a school outing.

The forestry authorities attached an experienced man to our group, who explained the situation. "The job we've got, girls, is to replant some large areas of forest that have been clear-cut. You'll be given a fresh supply of seedlings every day. I'll be coming for you at seven o'clock and taking you to the site. There I'll show you how to plant young conifers. I hope you like it here. And now goodbye till I fetch you tomorrow morning."

The following day we set off for the planting site at a brisk pace. It was all quite unreal. Terezín was forgotten.

All those fortifications and the uniformed SS men disappeared from our minds – even the war raging across Europe. Only the beautiful green trees remained, silent, peaceful and unearthly. They carried a whiff of eternity, quite detached from all that was going on around them. The smell of resin, pine-needles and moss was intoxicating.

We worked hard all day and sank into healthy sleep each evening in our bunks. How we loved it there. We regretted that we couldn't spend the rest of our days in this quiet paradise until the war was over. One day, after we came back from work, an unusual thing happened. One of the gendarmes came into our cabin, which he normally never did, and asked in a severe official tone:

"Is there a Fantlová Zdenka amongst you?"

I swallowed hard. Why would anybody be looking for me here? Could it have anything to do with my escaping from the transport group? It all looked rather alarming. I hesitated for a moment. My neighbour, who knew my name, looked at me questioningly. I realised there was no escape.

The gendarme stared hard at us all, and waited.

"Well," he repeated, "is the girl in question here or isn't she?"

"Yes, it's me," I sighed and half-raised my hand.

"Come with me, then," said the gendarme.

I staggered out as if never to return. When we arrived at the police hut he motioned me to go in. He followed me and shut the door behind us.

"Look," he said, "some middle-aged civilian turned up around mid-day and told us he'd heard a rumour going around that there were some girls from Terezín working here. And if there was a certain Fantlová Zdenka among them, as I now know there is, would we allow him to leave something here for her. He didn't give a name, said it didn't matter. So here it is. Take it back with you to Terezín when you return there in a couple of days."

Crossing over to the corner of the room he handed me a heavy case. "We have no objection to your having it," he said.

This was a quite unexpected turn of events. My fears evaporated and I now felt so deeply touched by the humanity and self-sacrifice involved that I could find no words. It could only have been one man, Matýsek, my father's old assistant, who had always been so fond of us, as we of him. He used to take me to school and called me Sumbalka. How heart-warming to know that there were good people around even in the worst of times.

I took the case back to our log-cabin and opened it up. It was full of treasures: clothes, underclothing, stockings, soap, bread, two tins of dripping, biscuits, and lump sugar. Everything he had managed to lay hands on. And it must have been an enormous expense, effort and sacrifice for him. Here in Křivoklát we weren't starving, but I gave each of the girls something.

When we left two days later the gendarmes and the forester came to say goodbye and wish us a safe journey. I arrived back in Terezín with my case looking as if I had just come from abroad. No one asked me any questions. My mother, brother and sister were all delighted, both to have me back and to see my case and everything inside it.

My gratitude to Matýsek knew no bounds.

27

"Can you cry, miss?"

Back in Terezín, I immediately resumed my place in the kitchen and was soon reaccustomed to the old routine and discipline. During my absence several of our group had been sent East. New people had taken their places among the kitchen staff, dishing out food and punching meal slips.

Among them was a pale young man in a belted raincoat and blue beret. He had big eyes and looked like sad Pierrot, the traditional Italian theatre character. I had no idea then of his name or what he had been doing before he came to Terezín. One day there were hundreds of people in the soup queue, impatient to be served. I was on duty, standing with my ladle at the ready and waiting for the *parták* to give the word. This pale young man stood there too with his punch for clipping the meal tickets.

Suddenly he turned to me and said, "Excuse me, miss. Can you cry?"

I wondered why I should be asked such an unusual question, but without much hesitation answered: "Mmm, yes, I can."

"Right, then. Come along to the Magdeburg barracks this evening to our play rehearsal. We're trying something new, our own cabaret, *Prince Confined-to-Bed*, something I wrote with a friend. My name's Josef Lustig."

I soon found out that Josef Lustig was an established actor and playwright, best known, despite his appearance, for comedy and satirical cabaret.

Such was my entrée to the world of the stage in Terezín.

28

Theatre in Terezín

The theatre made a modest, tentative start in Terezín, slinking in on tiptoe, as it were. Among the inmates were numerous well-known Czech actors, directors, stage designers, writers and artists, as well as professional musicians, conductors and composers. So there was no shortage of artistic talent.

Many people had a deep yearning to express themselves artistically, both in words and music, and the rest welcomed the results with gratitude as a compensation for their confinement. Every cultural event buoyed up their hopes and morale, and reinforced their faith in human values. Culture was a leftover from pre-war civilised life, but in these trying and uncertain conditions it acquired a deep new significance as well.

It all started with solo performances on the top floors of the barracks – sometimes poetry recitals, sometimes readings from whatever literature people had brought along in their suitcases. Later on came dramatic fragments involving several voices. The first efforts were cautious and faltering, as though the actors were testing the ice to see if it would bear their weight. The thought in everyone's mind was simply, "What will the Germans think?"

Surprisingly, the Germans had no objection at all to these innocent experiments. On the contrary, they gave official blessing to what they named *Kamaradenabende*, "friendly evenings." From that moment on, artistic activity in Terezín grew by leaps and bounds. Little stages with wings and curtains were constructed in the attics, then benches were set out in front of them – instant theatre! Some plays were imported from outside, some written by the inmates themselves. Theatrical companies were formed, sometimes with separate groups specialising in different genres. Directors were on tap, backdrops were painted and costumes made from whatever was available – sacking, bed sheets, paper and scraps of old clothing.

The same sort of thing happened with music. Instruments, sheet music and scores appeared from nowhere. Enough talent was discovered to assemble a jazz band, then a string quartet, a choir and even an entire orchestra.

Everyone gave of their best, whatever their ability, and for no reward at all.

There were no names in neon lights, no fame, no fortune – only the satisfaction of a job well done and the appreciation of a grateful audience. To this end professionals and amateurs worked hand in hand, free of envy or self importance.

29

Dancing under the gallows

I turned up punctually that evening at the Magdeburg barracks, feeling rather important and special now that I was moving in artistic circles.

Josef Lustig was standing on the stage, talking to his friend and collaborator, Jirí Spitz. Karel Kowanitz was with them too. He had written the lyrics of the songs that ran through the show. They had decided to base their cabaret on the style of the famous Voskovec and Werich partners, so that the Terezín Theatre would be a miniature version of the radical Liberated Theatre in Prague. The content would be allegorical. Between the scenes Lustig and Spitz, dressed as clowns, would deliver a topical commentary in front of the curtain, punctuated with songs set to the original theatre music, but with new lyrics of their own.

Their play *Prince Confined-to-Bed* was a fairy-tale allegory set in the reign of King Gumboil XII, featuring his son, Prince Confined-to-Bed, and his daughter, Princess Off-Duty. The palace scenes were done like a puppet play with jerky movements and squeaky voices, a take-off of the "puppet government" that ran the Terezín camp. The audience cheered wildly at every satirical scene or remark.

The action of the play was pretty simple. Prince Confined-to-Bed falls ill, is declared by his doctor unfit for work and hence for transport. But the wicked magician releases him from bed so that he can join the transport. At that point a young girl in the audience bursts into tears over the Prince's plight. Hearing this, the clowns invite her up on stage and assure her that the Prince is going to stay bedridden and everything will turn out all right.

I was supposed to take the part of the tearful girl. I promised to do my best.

Rehearsals proceeded, and at a given cue I had to sob quietly at first, then weep out loud. On the opening night they put me among the audience in the third row. No one took any notice of me and the play began. Every seat in the attic auditorium was filled.

But things went all wrong. When my cue came I began quietly sobbing and everyone around me tried to shut me up. "Shhh!" "Don't interrupt!" "For Christ's sake, be quiet!"

But I went on realistically howling and desperately waiting for the clowns to rescue me by saying, "Hang on! What's that young lady crying about?" and fetching me up on stage. Whereupon the audience would sigh with relief and realise it was all part of the action.

However, nothing of the kind happened. The clowns had decided to build up the tension. But meanwhile, the fire attendant in the doorway took action. With one leap he rushed up and started dragging me out as a disruptive element. Not wanting to spoil the play, I went on crying while hissing at him between my teeth, "I'm part of the play!"

That didn't impress him at all. "Oh yeah? Just come along quietly!"

At that moment a voice came from the stage, "Hang on! Why's that young lady crying?"

The fire attendant was impervious. His job was to keep law and order, and I was already halfway out the door.

There was now great commotion among the spectators, who were not sure what was going on. At the very last moment one of the clowns jumped down and hauled me back, to the audience's great relief. And mine.

It wasn't an easy role. Something different happened every night. At the second performance, on the given cue, I started sobbing and then crying out loud. Across the gangway an elderly man was sitting with a case on his lap, evidently a doctor. He jumped up, took out his instruments and was on the point of giving me a sedative injection for hysteria. Just in time, the actors on stage saw what was happening and came to my rescue.

Each evening there was some new incident. But word got around quickly and after a few days everyone in Terezín knew about this girl who cried in the audience. In the end, people started looking around long before my scene was due and laughing prematurely.

"Watch it now. That girl in the third row's going to start crying any moment, ho-ho-ho ..."

If it hadn't been for the transports to the East, still taking place at irregular intervals and hanging over our heads like swords of Damocles, we could almost have fancied we were living normal lives. The Germans began actively to support our cultural efforts and, at the same time, to exploit them for propaganda purposes. Hitler had "given the Jews an independent city", they claimed. True, we had more freedom of movement inside the fortified walls of Terezín than outside. But it was all a mirage.

They had their own definite plans for our future – and kept them strictly to themselves. They had condemned us to death, but allowed us to play and sing until the end.

Why shouldn't we? The smiles would soon be wiped from our faces.

So we all carried on, dancing under the gallows. And thus from the unlikely but supremely fertile soil of overcrowded Terezín, amid the wretched hunger, fear and constant deaths – but also amid hope and refusal to succumb to pain and humiliation – there arose an unprecedented theatrical and musical culture of the highest quality.

The Czech theatre in this camp was no mere entertainment or social distraction, but a living torch showing people the way ahead and lending them spiritual strength and hope. For many, a cultural experience became more important than a ration of bread.

I really felt at home amongst those actors and artists. On top of their eight-hour working day they threw themselves into acting, rehearsing, writing. Their ranks included many men and women of exceptional talent and ability who, no sooner had they arrived in Terezín, entered into its cultural life, stamping its plays and concerts with their individual genius and raising its creative standards to extraordinary heights.

One such man was Karel Švenk – writer, composer, choreographer, actor and clown. Something of a Czech Chaplin.

He was about twenty-five and his twinkling eyes, under bushy black brows, radiated energy. He wrote, acted and compèred his own cabaret. Unlike Lustig and Špitz with their domestic topics, Švenk's satires were markedly political In his first revue, *Long Live Life*, complete with mime and ballet, Švenk played the part of a persecuted clown.

What achieved overnight fame, however, was the closing song, which had a jolly march rhythm. It echoed the suppressed longings of every inmate, and we promptly adopted it as our Terezín anthem:

Where there's a will there's always a way
So hand in hand we start,
Whatever the trials of the day
There's laughter in our heart
Day after day we go on our way
From one place to another,
We're only allowed thirty words to a letter
But hey, tomorrow life starts again
And that's a day nearer to when we can pack
And leave for home with a bag on our back.
Where there's a will there's always a way
So hold hands now, hold them fast,
And over the ghetto's ruins we
Shall laugh aloud at last

And this is how we all honestly believed things would end up.

Švenk's second production, *The Last Cyclist*, had a clearly allegorical plot and a provocatively anti-Nazi message. The story was roughly this: All the madmen and psychopaths in some imaginary country rebel and escape from their asylums. After causing a public uproar they seize the reins of government. They are led by a ruler called the Rat. To find a scapegoat for all the misrule and shortages they have caused, they pick on one group of people who can be blamed for everything – cyclists.

Cyclists, they say, are the root of all evil and responsible for everything that has gone wrong. Cyclists are, moreover, a dangerous element backed by an international conspiracy. The country must get rid of them. A list of all cyclists has to be compiled, except for those who can prove that their ancestors over the last six generations were all pedestrians. The cyclists are caught and loaded on board a ship and taken to the Island of Horror.

Among the deportees is one Borivoj Abeles. Leaning over the railings he loses his balance and falls into the water. He starts swimming towards the nearest shore and thinks he is now safe. But the madmen see him, fish him out and lock him in a cage in the zoo, where he is exhibited as the Last Cyclist. But the Rat-dictator has other ideas. He orders the country to rid itself of this last cyclist. He is to be put into a rocket and shot off into the stratosphere. When everything is ready for take-off, the Rat and his female companion, the Lady, go on board with her staff to inspect the rocket. They grant Borivoj Abeles one last wish. He asks to be allowed a cigarette.

He strikes a match and absentmindedly, instead of lighting his cigarette, puts the match to the fuse of the rocket. The rocket hurtles off, along with the Rat and the Lady and her staff, while Borivoj stands watching it disappear into outer space.

The Last Cyclist somehow eluded German censorship, but its effect on the audience was like dynamite. However, its run was cut short. When the members of the Council of Elders came to see it, they were horror-struck by its obviously provocative allegory, and banned it.

Many of the inmates had already had a chance to enjoy the play, but many others were denied the pleasure. Its story became part of Terezín legend and the courageous Karel Švenk became a local hero.

30

Ben Akiba was no liar – or was he?

Over the course of 1943 it seemed that transports to the East had become considerably fewer and then come to a halt. Part of the explanation was that the German government had transferred one sector of its war production to Terezín and needed all available manpower. The sector in question involved laminating mica for military purposes. Wooden cabins were quickly erected for hundreds of workers, mostly women, who sat all day splitting sheets of mica.

The constant fear of being transported to the East suddenly abated and a period of apparent calm spread through Terezín. A rumour began to circulate that, according to reports from abroad, the German war front was retreating and the war would be over in two months. How eager we all were to believe this! But two months went by and the war still wasn't over. Hopes were then transferred to the next two months, and the next. So time went on and somehow one could always survive two months at a time.

The time seemed appropriate for some further theatrical experiments. Lustig and Spitz assembled a sizeable body of actors for a new play, *Ben Akiba Was No Liar – Or Was He?*

The play, or rather cabaret, features two clowns disputing the wisdom of the legendary Rabbi Ben Akiba in his famous pronouncement that "There is nothing new under the sun.

Everything has happened before."

The first clown sets out to convince his partner that every event is merely a repetition of some earlier one, albeit in different form and circumstances, so that there is really nothing new under the sun. To prove the point he transports him through time to a Roman arena where Christian prisoners are being thrown to the lions. One of the victims is Mordechai Pinkas. He tries to explain to the hungry lion that it is all a mistake, since he is a Jew and not a Christian at all. The lion sniffs him and finds no difference. Mordechai starts to negotiate and addresses the lion.

"Mr Leo, sir, Mr Levi, sir, be reasonable. I shouldn't be here at all, I'm Jewish." After a long argument he persuades the lion there has been an organisational mix-up and he is allowed to leave the arena.

"You see?" the second clown bursts in. "Now *that* has *never* happened before." So Ben Akiba *was* lying.

Between this scene and the next the clowns come to the front of the stage and start delving into old Czech history with a punning dialogue in the manner of the Voskovec and Werich interludes.

"Taking things from the very beginning, then, we have the ancestor of all Czechs, the Grand Ancestor, Cech, standing on Rípa Hill, stretching his arm out to the sun and declaring: This is the land overflowing with milk and mead – *tato zeme oplévá mlékem a strdim.*"

"Sorry to interrupt you … really sorry … but could you please tell me exactly what this 'mead' is?"

"I *beg* your pardon? You've never heard of mead?"

"Terribly sorry … but honestly … I never really *have* understood what 'mead' is."

"You ought to be ashamed. Everyone knows what mead is, any child can tell you."

"Any child, yes … yes … but me, I've no idea."

"Have you never seen it written up in front of a restaurant? Like Today's special, sour mead'?"

"Not really, no."

"For goodness sake, man, how can I explain? Mead is simply … well …mead … isn't it? So let's not waste any more time and get on with the next stage in Czech history. The ancient Czechs were a very advanced people who burnt their dead and put their ashes *do uren umne zdobených*, into artistically decorated urns."

Second clown (pretending he heard the phonetically identical *do uren u mne zdobených*, urns decorated in my house): "Is that so, now? I never realised you did your business in urns as well as in textiles!"

"No, you've got me wrong. I said *umne*, artistically like."

"Oh, well, if it was done in your place I've no doubt it was very artistic."

The wordplay continued endlessly and the audience loved it. The "mead" episode was particularly successful and people were forever buttonholing each other when they met and repeating parts of the dialogue. Two venerable members of the Council of Elders were even overheard conversing in the corridor:

"I say, very amusing that bit about 'mead' in the Ben Akiba piece, eh?"

"Indeed."

"But tell me, professor, what exactly is mead?"

"You don't mean to say you don't know?"

And so it went on, all around the town. No one knew what mead was.

The next scene was set on Olympus, where the gods were holding council around a table, arguing and failing to agree about anything. Zeus was in the chair, trying to moderate. Their quarrels were meant to echo the divisions within both the Council of Elders and the German political leadership. I played the part of Aphrodite. Instead of just being pretty and quietly seducing all the gods, she kept on interfering, correcting the others and disrupting the proceedings.

Scene Three was set in Heaven, where the Empress Maria Theresa and her son Joseph are sitting on a cloud, looking down through a telescope. What should come swimming into their field of view but Terezín, the town they had founded as a fortress against the Prussians. They look harder and harder but the place seems so unfamiliar. What can have happened to it, they speculate.

Then suddenly two Jewish souls come floating up, straight from Terezín, and offer to give the empress and her son a detailed account of events down there. But their majesties reject it out of hand. From which the Second Clown deduces that what is now happening in the fortress is truly unprecedented. So Ben Akiba *was* lying.

One of the theme songs running through the cabaret was written by František Kowanitz to the tune of Jaroslav Jezek's famous satirical song, "Civilisation":

A certain ruler issued a decree
As we can read in any History,
Fearing attack by enemies afar
To build a fortress city like a star.
To make invasion really difficult
He had a ring of mighty earthworks built,
With creeks and coves to each redoubt
And moats and ditches roundabout
Plus soldiery within the walls
To fire their cannon balls.
The citizens were super posh,
Prime pork and haggis was their nosh,
They loved to sing pub songs, and those
Were meant to terrify their foes.
But many years have passed since then,
The world has somewhat changed its face,

And since the town inspired no dread
Word came that those of a certain race
Must all wear stars and live inside
By thousands, filling every shop, wall, inn,
Barracks and café, till there was no space,
No food, and anyone was glad
To eat the odd potato-skin.
Rations were short because there was a crisis,
No booze, no cash for paying silly prices,
When suddenly the town's true role
In a new light was seen
To serve as propaganda both
In newspapers and on the screen.

In view of the last-mentioned revelation
There now arose a new organisation,
New insights and new points of view,
New parties and new leaders too.
All labour was deployed by Hundertschaften,
A Raumwirtschaft saw to each inmate's comfort,
Verteilungsstellen issued them fine clothes,
Bettenbau got them snug asleep at night,
Entwesung saw to bodily hygiene, and
Freizeitgestaltung put their souls aright.

All the organisations with German names mentioned in the last verse really existed and saw to it that life went on in Terezín in as orderly a way as possible.

The *Hundertschaft* was a labour unit of one hundred men.

The *Raumwirtschaft* allocated living space in the billets.

The *Verteilungsstelle* collected clothes from those who died, sorted them and "sold" them in shops set up for the purpose.

Bettenbau was a carpentry shop which made bunks, as well as partitions and "furniture" for the élite in their penthouses and cubby-holes.

Entwesung was the de-lousing and disinfecting station. The Germans were obsessed by the danger of epidemics of any kind.

Freizeitgestaltung – "leisure structuring" – was a new department within the self-governing administration which had arisen during the great cultural upsurge and dealt with all its requirements. It authorised new sites (mainly in the attics) for plays and concerts, organised scientific and literary talks, assigned rehearsal time to pianists on the two available pianos, allocated materials for scenery, and printed theatre and concert programmes and tickets. It was responsible for the choice of dramatic material for performance.

Freizeitgestaltung was also concerned with leisure time sports, of which the most popular was football. This was played even in the most cramped barracks courtyards. Every male barracks had its own team, so one would find, for example, *Sudeten* trying to get the better of *Hannover*. Matches were fought with as much passion as if international trophies were at stake, and around the hastily prepared playing grounds the galleries were packed with fans on every floor.

Music occupied an even larger place than the theatre in our cultural life. Terezín was awash with outstanding musical performers, conductors and composers. The famous Prague conductor Karel Ancerl, who used to stir the soup beside me in the kitchen during his working hours, organised a string quartet in his free time and, later on, a complete orchestra.

The composer Hans Krása, already established before the war, made his name in Terezín with his unique children's opera *Brundibár*. This was a musical fairy story played and sung by children in the camp between eight and twelve years old. It was rehearsed and performed countless times both for young and adult audiences in the Sokol hall. The story was simple and topical:

Two little children, Pepíček (Joey) and Anna, find that their mother is ill. They would like to bring her some milk, but they have no money. So they decide to sing in the streets in the hope of earning enough to buy some. They sing their best and passers-by throw coins into their cap. But then along comes the wicked organ grinder Brundibár, who tries to stop them and steals their cap with all the money. With the help of some animals – a dog, a cat and a sparrow – they overcome Brundibár and chase him off. Justice has been done and the piece ends with the children's chorus

Nad Brundibárem jsme vyhrály, my jsme se nebály.
We fought old Brundibár and won, because we weren't afraid.

The little performers and their audiences were equally thrilled. I remember squeezing into the hall where seats and all standing room were crammed full. Lovely, healthy, talented kids they were, and all of them prisoners. Their eyes shone with excitement at the fall of wicked Brundibár.

This was in September 1943.

Soon afterwards came the order to resume transports. Most of the children who had so merrily performed in *Brundibár* were sent to their fate in the East. End of fairy tale.

Several of our *Ben Akiba* cast went off too and we had to suspend the cabaret. In the end we were never able to perform it again because our treasured Josef Lustig's tuberculosis suddenly got worse. He lay in the sick-bay in Kavalírka barracks. I used to visit him as often as I could and, as a little treat, take him part of my own ration from the kitchen. There were no medicines. He knew he would never live to see his home again.

When I was sitting on his bed one day, Josef said to me, "You remember the first time I ever spoke to you, and asked you 'Can you cry, miss?' Well, when I die, don't cry. If you survive it all, you must tell people how we kept the show going in Terezín."

Two days later he died.

When I went to see him they were just carrying him out of the room, wrapped in a sheet.

Our group now dissolved, having completed its mission: to use satire to convey the truth, while trying to give the audiences some moral support and hope.

It was not long after Lustig's death that his inseparable colleague, fellow writer and actor Jirí Spitz, was also taken off somewhere to the East. I sat with him until the early hours before he was loaded onto the cattle truck, helping him sort out the few things he was taking with him. We speculated about where he might be going. We had just had time to sing Švenk's Terezín anthem to ourselves:

Where there's a will there's always a way
So hold hands now, hold them fast,
And over the ghetto's ruins we
Shall laugh aloud at last

And then he was off.

In the darkness of Terezín our cabaret had been like a sparkler on a Christmas tree that lights up and dazzles for a brief moment, then suddenly goes out. But everyone who saw it retained in his mind's eye the memory of its short, vivid existence.

31

Life goes on

Miraculously, my own family, except for Father, managed to hold together. My brother Jírka had been on shift work in the bakery for some time and whenever he got a special ration he would bring some back as a treat for Mother.

Mother was still in the Hamburg billet we had been assigned when we arrived, but alone now with my sister Lydia. I had moved into my cubby-hole, my little train compartment, and came back to see Mother whenever I had a free moment. She was sad and anxious.

One day our grandmother was put on the transport list. There was no appeal. Alone and sick as she was, she had to go East. God knows why the Germans could not have let the elderly, at least, stay on in Terezín instead of shifting them in these insufferable transport trains to unknown destinations where they would die anyway. It was a bitter, cruel leave-taking.

Soon another transport included the room leader of Mother's billet, so that a successor had to be elected. They chose Mother. This was her salvation. She now had plenty to worry about: maintaining order, keeping the billet quiet and tidy, dividing up the bread ration, and so forth.

My sister worked with other youngsters on the ramparts, growing tomatoes for the German garrison.

But they weren't allowed to touch them and they were very strictly checked. As she was working apart from me, we didn't see much of each other. Sometimes she sneaked into the audience to see a play I was in. I was always glad to see her, although I noticed that she seemed to have more interest in Petr, a boy who was operating the lights, than she was in my performance.

Then one day the news spread that a thousand male volunteers were being taken on for work outside Terezín, in the Kladno coal mines. My brother signed up. Mother protested, just as she had when I went tree planting in Krivoklát. But he went all the same, with a large group of young men. At the appointed time they all returned to Terezín.

Mother sighed with relief to see him back. He himself would much rather have stayed in Kladno, but he had no choice.

Time moved on. We had grown accustomed to the Terezín routine and forgotten our old homes. In fact we no longer felt we were even entitled to remember them. Other things were more important, like not getting listed for transport and staying alive until the war ended. Surely sometime it must end.

Daily life in Terezín was a continuous kaleidoscope. New transports arrived and were sorted out into work groups, old people died, the artistic crowd put on plays and concerts, transports left for the East, lovers hid where they could, more people died, orphans survived on their own in children's blocks ... We waited and waited, trying to hold on until the end.

———✦———

I was missing Arno badly. He had been gone for nearly two years. Where might he be? Was he alone, or with his brother? What was he doing? Was he in a camp? Working outside, or in a factory? How was he being treated? Was he in good health and determined to hang on to the end? After all, we were going to find each other as soon as the war was over and start a happy new life amidst peace and affection – and forget there had ever been a war.

But no answers came to my questions. Here and there words like "Auschwitz" or "Birkenau" were mentioned but no one knew anything definite. It was all guesswork.

Among the Terezín inmates was an old clairvoyant who claimed to know what had happened to those who went East.

When she sought inspiration she had to hold something in her hand that had belonged to the lost one. I went to consult her with the ring Arno had made, the one tangible thing that linked us together. I trembled to hear what she might say. She sat in her chair with her eyes shut, turning the ring in her hand. My heart thumped as I waited for her answer.

"I can't find him anywhere," she said softly. "All I can see is the letter 'T.' Nothing else."

I went off, rather relieved that she had not told me anything definite or devastating. I remained convinced that, wherever he was, Arno would find in himself the strength to survive.

32

The Potemkin Village façade

It was in the spring of 1944 that the German leadership invited an international commission to visit Terezín and see for themselves the "paradise" which the Führer himself had designed for the Jews. The local command accordingly ordered a campaign of embellishment. Feverish preparations were initiated.

So that the city should not appear overcrowded, 7,000 wretched inhabitants were immediately sent off to the East.

The streets and squares that the commission would be passing through had to be thoroughly spruced up. A café was constructed on the main square where selected inmates could be seen drinking coffee and eating cakes while a jazz orchestra, the Ghetto Swingers, played for their pleasure. Grass was ordered to be sown, and flowering shrubs planted around the edge of the town, where benches would be set up for people to sit and exchange lively, jolly conversation. An orchestra would play in a brand new pavilion in the centre of the town.

Paths were cleaned up for selected prisoners to take their leisurely strolls. New playgrounds with swings and other delights were to be laid out for the children.

The façades of houses in designated streets were given a fresh coat of whitewash and their windows fitted with pretty curtains. Shop windows were quickly cleared of those who had been billeted in them and who had now been dispatched eastward. Their old quarters were soon tastefully decorated with goods removed from the luggage of new arrivals.

Once I passed one such window being rearranged by the well-known stage artist and designer Honza Zelenka.

"Hello, Honza," I said, "what are you doing here?"

He took a few steps back and eyed his work critically. "Just adding a few meaningless touches," he answered, with a dismissive wave of the hand.

A model troupe of pretty girls, including my sister Lydia, were ordered to cross the square carrying rakes over their shoulders and strolling to a tune, as if finishing a day's gardening.

Inmates from the children's blocks were to be seen crowding around Lagerkommandant Rahm, the German officer in charge of Terezín. He would hand them out tins of sardines while they recited well-rehearsed lines: "Oh, not sardines again, Uncle Rahm!"

The day before the commission was due, a squad of women was assembled with brooms, cloths and pails of water, who then knelt and scrubbed the pavements until they shone like mirrors. We weren't allowed to walk on them that day.

The eminent visitors arrived as planned and drove in open cars through the specially beautified streets and squares. Everything went perfectly. Haggard figures sat on the new benches, melancholy faces stared from the cafés. Karel Ancerl conducted his orchestra in the concert hall, and in the Sokol hall a choir directed by Raphael Schächter sang Verdi's *Requiem*. The international commission left thoroughly convinced of the authenticity of the Terezín paradise. Immediately after the inspection several new thousand-strong transports were assembled to leave for the East, including most of the children who, only a few days before, had been so realistically thanking Kommandant Rahm for their sardines.

33

The Czech theatre carries on

The theatrical world of Terezín could never have functioned without the activity behind the scenes by the enormously experienced and ingenious František Zelenka. Architect and stage designer by training, he had made his name long before the war with his avant-garde sets for leading Prague stages, including the Liberated Theatre.

As soon as he came to Terezín in 1943, he threw himself into theatre work, which was enjoying its golden age at that time. He had his own workshop where backdrops were set up and painted, stage properties constructed and costumes designed and created. He had to make bricks without straw. He used any material that came his way – paper, sawdust, rags, empty tins, old sheets – and achieved miracles with it. His skill was responsible for the brilliant design of the children's opera *Brundibár* and of the stage productions that followed.

He worked closely with that most able of directors, Gustav Schorsch, who had been an assistant director of the National Theatre in Prague before coming to Terezín. Schorsch was a theatrical purist, pedagogue and theoretician of the old school and would tolerate no departure from the highest standards. Using a group of young Prague professional players and Zelenka's designs, he put on a production of Gogol's *The Marriage* that would have won acclaim anywhere in the world.

In his "spare time" Gustav organised recitals of Czech poetry and held a seminar for young actors. After the great success of *The Marriage* he started working on a play by Griboyedov but had to abandon it after a few rehearsals, when some of his cast were sent East. The same fate attended his planned production of Shakespeare's *Twelfth Night* after his remaining actors were swallowed up in the new wave of transports.

After the dispersal of Lustig's cabaret group, the few of us who remained had been transferred to other projects. One of these was Štech's *Tretí Zvonení* (*Third Time Lucky*), and soon after that the actress Vlasta Schönová started rehearsals for František Langer's comedy *Velbloud Uchem Jehly* (*A Camel Through The Eye Of A Needle*).

It was the mere coincidence of both texts turning up in Terezín that made it possible to produce these two light-hearted plays, familiar from pre-war days. They were given a great welcome and for one evening, at least, revived memories of happier times in better places.

34

Esther

It was some time in 1943 that the writer-director Norbert (Nora) Frýd and the composer Karel Reiner arrived in Terezín. Each had worked in his own field with E.F. Burian and his avante garde *Divadlo D*, Theatre D, in Prague. Nora Frýd brought with him in his luggage the text of a biblical folk play, *Esther*, which had been rehearsed under Burian but never reached the stage. The Terezín theatre world seemed to have been waiting for these two men, who both got down to work immediately. Frýd took on the production and Reiner composed original music for it. He would sit at his little piano in front of the stage extemporising half-tone melodies as the play proceeded.

František Zelenka in turn took on the staging and costume designs. They made a happy trio. *Esther* was a contrast to all the other plays staged in Terezín. For a start, it was written in verse, and in near-medieval Czech at that.

The production completely dispensed with realism and was imaginatively stylised. The story itself, telling how Queen Esther saved her Jewish tribe from certain annihilation, was deeply meaningful for Terezín and its inhabitants.

The plot was simple and straightforward. The play is set in a land ruled by the mighty Persian King Ahasuerus, whose loyal servant and palace gatekeeper is the Jew, Mordecai.

One day Mordecai overhears two chamberlains plotting to kill the king. To save his master from certain death he reports the plot to him. The king orders the chamberlains executed, and promises his servant a rich reward for saving his life. Mordecai, however, declines any reward, continuing to render faithful service. The king then arranges a great banquet for his subjects to which he invites his wife, Queen Vashti. But she refuses to attend and the King, angered by her disobedience, removes her crown and has her barred from the palace.

Then, summoning a parade of young virgins, he chooses the one he likes best, Esther. This Esther is also Jewish and a niece of Mordecai. Meanwhile, out of generosity and relief at escaping death, the king has appointed his counsellor, Prince Haman, as minister with unlimited powers. Both Haman and his wife Zeresh are greedy for wealth, power and fame. Following his promotion, Haman now orders that all the king's servants and subjects should pay homage to *him*. But Mordecai refuses; he will only bow before the king.

Haman is furious at this impudence and conceives a plan to hang Mordecai and wipe out his entire tribe, so purging the Persian land of all Jews. In no time Haman has a gallows erected in the palace courtyard.

When he hears of this, Mordecai begins to moan. Esther, learning of Mordecai's sadness, decides to appeal to the king to save her people. The king accepts her plea and, incensed at Haman's arrogance and unjust spite, has him hanged on the new gallows, refusing all pleas for mercy. So all ends well, his subjects rejoice and wish King Ahasuerus glory and long life.

Rehearsals went ahead at a feverish pace and the production began to take shape. Out of nothing, Zelenka produced sets that would have done credit to any theatre of international standing. The entire backdrop was a semicircle of "straw" to lend pastoral colour. There were three separate tents on the stage with sackcloth curtains. Sitting in each one was a leading character: the king in the middle tent, the queen on the right and Mordecai in the left-hand tent. The Narrator, stick in hand, walks around in front of the tents and tells the story.

Then with his stick he pulls aside the curtain of one tent, announcing: "And the king said …" or the Queen, or Mordecai, as the plot developed.

Zelenka dreamt up quite ravishing costumes. King Ahasuerus was put into a white sheet, cut out in the middle for his head, and empty tins were sewn onto the bottom hem so that they tinkled when he walked.

"When you cross the stage," Zelenka explained, "I want to hear the cans rattling against each other."

On his head the king wore a cut-out paper crown, with blobs of auburncoloured sawdust stuck onto his head and forearms. He carried a whipstock in his hand, and looked very impressive.

Zelenka dressed Haiman's wife Zeresh in loose-flowing multi-coloured robes. "I want you" he said, "to look like some figure flying through a window display in Ascher's House of Silk on Mustek in the middle of Prague." Which is just what she did look like.

I played the part of Queen Vashti. Zelenka dressed me in two sheets sewn together, the inside one white, the outer dyed black. The outer one had large peacock eyes cut out of it, so that the white undersheet showed through. His instructions were simple: "When you walk along the stage and the clothes flap around you, I want you to look like a baroque angel over a grave."

And thus it appeared. He was full of ingenious ideas and humorous fancies.

At last the rehearsals were over. Each of us knew the words and music to perfection. The play was a great success and everything went well each night. Then, one evening, I hatched a devilish plot. I'd had a heated argument before the performance with Karel Kavan, who played the king. I was sure that he was in the wrong and I was determined at any price to punish him by spoiling his performance.

I didn't quite know how to achieve this when suddenly a way occurred to me of diverting the whole drift of the play. In my first scene the king's minister comes up to me and says:

We are sent by his Majesty
To bid you come and join him

Whereupon the queen, who has already turned down his invitation to the banquet, answers:

I told you once I would not come,
To change my mind I see no need.
So once again I tell you, No,
I'll not, however hard he plead.

The minister goes off to tell the king of her decision. He is furious:

Lo, now my anger doth wax great
So take the crown from off her head,
Have her without the palace led.

The minister duly returns to the queen, removes her crown and bans her from the court. She paces to and fro, singing dolefully:

Alas for my great misery
The gods have quite forsaken me.
Where can I seek a friend
Now that my fortune's turned?
My crown is gone from me
And I on petty grounds
Am stripped of royalty.
Now must I to the woods
My life with beasts to spend
And make my home with them
Till life draws to its end.

Her song over, the queen leaves the palace. Curtain. End of Act One.

But on the night in question things went differently. The minister as usual comes to tell the queen that the king wants her at the banquet, and she should go with him now. At this point something clicked in my mind, and instead of refusing the invitation I answered in impeccable Old Czech:

Na královské porucení
uciním tak bez prodleni

In other words,

If the King so desires of me
I'll meet His wishes instantly

Then I dutifully went over to the kings tent.

Kavan had quite a shock when he saw me coming, as he had no words appropriate to the situation. So he desperately continued with the original text, saying how I had to be punished for my disobedience. My crown was removed, I crossed the stage, sang my doleful song and exited. Curtain.

I don't know what the audience made of it all. The king had invited her to the feast, she had accepted, and then been thrown out for her pains. Nora Frýd, however, was quite clear in his mind. He rushed up to the stage from the back row, shouting, "You really screwed it up, didn't you? You silly cow!"

He was very angry, justifiably so. I was hauled in front of the *Freizeit. gestaltung* committee, who gave me a drubbing for unprofessional behaviour. I apologised profusely to Nora and to Karel Kavan. And the show went on.

Like everything else, this little episode soon became the talk of the town.

———❖———

The *Esther* production, however well rehearsed and well received, finally fell victim to another series of transports. Several of the cast were taken off and the end was inevitable. With a heavy heart Nora told us he could not embark on fresh rehearsals with new actors. So that was the end of *Esther* in the little Magdeburg theatre.

But it was certainly a vintage production and retains a lasting place in the memories of the participants and of those spectators who had the chance to see it.

35

Georges Dandin

After the collapse of *Esther*, another director, Otakar Ruzicka, decided to put on the Molière comedy *Georges Dandin*. This only needed a small cast and I was assigned the part of the society lady Madame de Sottenville, starchly buttoned-up and with monocle permanently poised.

The rehearsals went badly and Ruzicka gave up. He was succeeded by Zelenka who was willing to take on directing as well as stage management. Production was transferred to the larger and better equipped stage on the top floor of the Dresden barracks, where there was room for a larger audience too. But despite these advantages the play was a flop. Whether it was the fault of the production or the weakness of the play itself, Molière and his subject didn't fit into the Terezín of those years.

So even though none of the cast was lost to the transports this time, the play closed.

I now found myself with evenings free and was finally able to enjoy one of the many concerts that Terezín was so well provided with. I chose a piano concert by Alice Herz-Sommerová, who was playing all of the Chopin

Études without a break. Her virtuosity transported listeners from wretched, starving Terezín to a different world and a different epoch. Sitting on that wooden bench I listened spellbound. It was an unforgettable evening.

Among the inmates were many professional musicians: concert leaders and soloists, composers, singers and conductors. Karel Ancerl had his little orchestra. Conductor Rafael Schächter assembled another opera chorus for a performance of *The Bartered Bride* that made the audience cry. There was an outstanding young pianist and composer, Gideon Klein; also, Viktor Ullman, professor of musical theory, who wrote a striking modern opera while he was in Terezín: *Císar z Atlan-tidy* (*The Emperor of Atlantis*).

This opera had a topical text with a political edge, written by young Peter Kien, which was bound to strike the German censors as provocative. Though rehearsals had been completed, it was banned and never saw a performance. But the plot is worth retelling:

An imaginary country is ruled by the cruel emperor Überall – "Overall" – who wages war against everyone. The slaughter is pitiless. Thousands die. Death himself cannot stand the sight of it any longer and informs the tyrant that he is going on strike. People stop dying and just crawl around with as much strength as they can muster. There are hordes of them, and constantly their numbers increase.

The emperor summons Death and begs him to resume his duties and allow people to die. Death accepts his pleading, but on one condition only – that the dictator is the first to die. End of opera. If only it would come true!

36

Terezín is wound up

Autumn 1944, and still the war went on. Hope alternated with despair. Even though news filtered through that the German army was retreating before the might of the Russian colossus and Anglo-American air power, all this seemed academic. It had no connection with us. On the contrary, the clouds over Terezín were growing ever darker.

The end came suddenly. Terezín was to be closed, the fate of its inmates thereby sealed for good. The orders read: "5,000 men to report for transport tomorrow, a further 3,000 the day after."

The streets were suddenly transformed into running rivers of people. All was bustle and excitement. Knots of inmates gathered to discuss the impending changes and swap guesses. But no one could say where we were all bound, or why. The town changed its character overnight, with everyone rushing to collect cases and rucksacks, find food for the journey, deliver last-minute messages. Quick, quick, for tomorrow we go. The transport department became a teeming anthill.

The Germans in charge announced that all they needed at the moment was fit young men to set up another temporary camp. Meanwhile, their families, wives and children would remain safe in Terezín. It all sounded very uncertain, but there was no avoiding their orders.

My brother came to say a hasty goodbye to my mother, sister and me, where we had quickly gathered in my mother's billet in Hamburg. The fact that 5,000 men were to go alleviated the sense of personal tragedy. In all the rush there was no time for brooding. As a single man my brother was at least spared the worry of those who were parting from wives and children, as so many were – hugging and kissing them and having no idea whether they would ever see them again.

"Don't worry about me, Mother," he said. "There are plenty of us, we're young and we can stand a lot. Anyway, the war will be over soon, it can't last much longer. I'll send you word if I can. If not, we'll all meet again at home when the war's finished."

We all gave him our bread rations and three fingers of margarine for the journey, and kissed him goodbye. Early next day he was taken off with the others in sealed cattle trucks.

After that the town never recovered its normal mood. Further transports, 2,500 strong, followed at short intervals. The whole business of running the town was in disarray. With so many able people disappearing from the top positions, an effort had to be made to replace them, but it was no easy task. People still had to be fed, the sick to be looked after, corpses to be cremated, and administration to be maintained. All the name files had to be right so that the Germans could check them. Everyone found their workload redoubled.

As always, there was no information about where those thousands of men had been sent. Rumours began to circulate that they were not being used to make a new camp at all, but had been carted off to a concentration camp called Auschwitz-Birkenau. There were no further details. The wives who had been left behind waited impatiently for some news, however meagre, to come from their husbands. But nothing came. Not a line. Silence.

Amid the ensuing tension came the announcement, virtually an order, that the German High Command in its kindness and humanity was offering all those women whose husbands had been taken away the opportunity to go and join them in the interest of family unity. Those who wished to volunteer for this purpose must do so that very same day.

No one hesitated. They signed up to the last woman. Crowds of women and children besieged the registration department for permission to travel voluntarily in the wake of their men folk. In the queues standing there until nightfall the mood was one of joy at the chance to rejoin their husbands.

There were sceptics in the camp who had had secret information from outside. "It's all a German trick," they warned, "a scheme for getting helpless people onto the eastward transports with minimum fuss. Don't volunteer and don't take your children! You'll never see your men again anyway!"

But the cynics were dismissed as prophets of doom and no one took their warnings seriously. All the women, with their children, who volunteered to go and join their husbands, even though they were not told where, left two days later. That was the last that was ever heard of them.

The population of Terezín was thinning out visibly. No new inward transports were arriving, but the outward ones were leaving almost daily with thousands of people. None of us now had any illusions of being left here in relative safety. We were just waiting for our turn to come. We didn't have to wait long.

37

Auschwitz-Birkenau

October 15, 1944 was a dismal autumn Sunday. Up until then, Sundays had been like any other day; but this one was different. It was the day we were summoned to join the eastward transport. The strip of pink paper with your name and number stared you in the face; a simple, brief label hiding your fate, as though in invisible writing.

A picture flashed through my mind of a country fair in the small town we had lived in before the war, where a parrot took horoscope cards out of a box with its beak for people to see what fate has in store for them. If they didn't like what they read they could tear the card up and go home. I was holding my fortune-slip in my hand now, but it told me nothing about the future. It kept its secret. I couldn't throw it away. I had to take it into the train with me and wait for destiny to unfold before my eyes.

My family was all ready for the journey – or rather what remained of my family – Mother, my sister and myself. My brother had been taken off a week before, Grandmother shortly before that, and my father had already been in prison for four years.

Terezín had been dealt a staggering blow. All the actors, directors, musicians and conductors, all the men of art, had received their summons to join the transport. Gustav

Schorch, director; Franta Zelenka, stage designer; Hans Krása and Viktor Ullman, composers; Gideon Klein, pianist; Raphael Schächter and Karel Ançerl, conductors. These and many others: fifteen hundred in all.

We were only allowed to take the barest necessities with us.

The Germans themselves handled the administration of the transports. Cattle trucks were waiting for us on the siding. We stood in the rain all night on the courtyard with our luggage by our sides so as to be ready when our names were called. They counted us over and over again so that no one was missing and the figures tallied.

Finally, in the early morning of 17 October, we climbed into the trucks and moved off. Where to? No idea. Only fear and uncertainty remained, a weird step into the darkness with nothing before one's eyes. The trucks were bolted and sealed from the outside. There were no windows. The air was clammy and hard to breathe. Those who could, squeezed onto the few wooden benches; the rest squatted on the floor. We were in for a long and appalling journey. Two buckets served the whole truck for sanitation. When nature called, and self-control ran out, people had to forget modesty, consideration and civilised norms. German rule, we saw, had reduced us to sub-human standards.

There were some 130 of us in our truck, including little children who were thirsty and kept crying. The old folk sitting on the floors propped themselves against the sides. Some of them were praying, some had given up hope. Three people in our truck died before we reached our destination.

Opposite me sat the same Raphael Schächter, who had been the prime mover of musical activities in Terezín. Holding his mess-tin in his hand he took his last bread ration from his knapsack, a tin of sardines (sheer luxury, and hard currency in Terezín) from one pocket, and a spoon from the other. He passed the whole lot over to me, and said, "Break the bread into my tin, would you, then open the sardines and mix the whole lot together. It's going to be my last supper."

He said this in the decisive tone of a man going to the gallows who has been allowed one last wish. Why, I wondered, is he giving up just now? Has he an inkling of worse to come?

He ate the food with relish, and his last supper it probably was. For suddenly, after twenty-nine endless hours in that train, we saw the station sign: AUSCHWITZ-BIRKENAU. We had arrived. The train came to a halt.

As soon as they opened the doors, noise and confusion broke out. Uniformed guards holding dogs on their leashes, shouted "*Raus! Raus!*" – "Out! Out!" – and aimed random blows with their truncheons. Not having stood up for so long, people's legs gave way when they tried to jump out, and they simply collapsed onto the ground.

There was no platform where the train had stopped, merely the end of the siding, leading nowhere. It was the end of the journey, then. Was it the end of us? The end of living? Who could say?

"*Gepäck im Wagen liegen lassen, nichts mitnehmen!*" screamed the guard.

"Leave all luggage behind, and make it snappy!" "*Raus! Raus! Schnell! Los!*" "Quick! Out! Out!" He used his boot to make his point. I jumped down to help Mother out of the truck; my sister was already beside me. Most of those around me were terrified and bewildered, like people roused from sleep at midnight, at a loss to know what was going on. But Mother had sized up the situation in her own way and said to us quietly, "We must keep tight hold of each other now, so that we don't get separated." She took my sister's hand.

I took a deep gulp of air. It smelled of smoke, with a curious sweetish tang, like scorched meat. There must be a slaughterhouse nearby, I thought, where they're burning cattle bones and offal. No other explanation occurred to me.

All around, as far as the eye could see, were low, narrow, windowless wooden huts, surrounded and separated from each other on all sides by high fences of electrified barbed wire, with tall watch-towers at intervals. The ground was covered in deep sticky mud, with great puddles of water.

At this point I spotted the first prisoners. They wore striped uniforms, with numbered squares on their backs and queer, frightened expressions in their eyes. They went everywhere on the trot, even when carrying heavy loads. They were always followed by guards with truncheons who drove them on whenever they slipped in the mud.

On the other side of the railway line, again surrounded by barbed wire, was a women's camp. The inmates at that moment were standing silently in five columns. They were all wearing extraordinary torn clothes, or rags, were either barefoot or shod in huge wooden clogs, and had no hair on their heads. They looked scarcely human, more like creatures from another world.

Who on earth can they be, I wondered. What country have they come from? What are they doing here?

They stood there silently, not moving, but with horror in their eyes. Up and down the columns strode an SS woman guard with a whip. Where on earth was I? What is this place? I had never seen or read about anything like it; no one had prepared us for such a scene, that a place like could exist. I felt as if I had fallen into some deep abyss and strayed into an unknown, terrifying underworld where devilish powers held sway, and there was no way out.

Suddenly, quite unexpectedly, a revelation shot through me like a flash of lightning, which, in a hundredth of a second, can illuminate the whole night countryside and show you where you are.

The revelation took the form of a voice. From where,

who knows? It spoke to me firmly and distinctly: "Now it will be a matter of naked life. Death reigns supreme here … You are in mortal danger, girl … but if you are lucky enough not to be killed, you have enough strength in you to survive … hard though it will be."

These words calmed me down. I took a deep breath and sensed that someone or something, somewhere or other, was holding a protective arm over me. My fear dropped away.

"Just keep calm," Father had said, when the Gestapo were taking him away. "Remember, calmness is strength."

At this moment one of the guards roared out a command: "*Vorwärts! Los! Marsch!*" – "Move on! March!" – and started hitting out with his truncheon at anyone within reach. The conductor Karel Ancerl was in line in front of me, holding in his arms a little boy of about a year, who must have been born in Terezín. His wife was next to him. An SS guard pushed in between them, snatched the child from him, thrust it into the wife's arms and gave Karel a kick that sent him sprawling in the mud.

Amid general confusion the crowd moved into marching order. Without our luggage now, we staggered on for more than a kilometre, carried by the momentum of the human river around us. In the row behind me was a young mother with a curly-haired little blonde girl of about four. The child held on to her mother with her left hand, while her right held a doll in a white dress with red polka-dots.

"Where are we going to, mummy?"

"To see Grandmother"

"Grandmother?" crowed the girl. "Oh, good! Is she expecting us?"

"Yes."

"I'm so thirsty, mummy. Will Grandmother have some milk for us?"

"Yes."

"Shall we be there soon?"

"Yes, darling. Quite soon." And the girl skipped with delight.

Finally we reached our destination. There were three SS officers standing with legs astride at the end of the path in skin-tight uniforms, with skull-and-crossbones emblems on their caps and jackboots polished to shine like mirrors. They looked sternly ahead. The one in the middle, wearing gloves, was dividing the column in two. He gestured leisurely with his forefinger to each arrival to go left or right. "*Links! Links! Links! Rechts! Links! Links! Rechts!*"

It was a quick process. Within a few minutes he had separated 1,500 women, men and children into two groups. Left. Right. Like a strange fork in the road, with no time for queries or farewells. All I could see was that the old, the sick and women with children were being sent to the left, the young and fit to the right. The Ancerls were just in front of me. With one wave of his hand the SS officer split them apart. Karel was directed right, his wife and child left. We did not know then that right meant life and left death. Now it was our turn. My mother, myself, and my sister between us.

Mother's expression was baleful. I looked the officer in the face. He was a handsome man, not evil-looking, though his clear blue eyes had a glint of cold steel.

"*Links*" – "Left" – he said to my mother, without a thought.

And with the same equanimity, "*Rechts*" – "Right" – to me.

To my sister he said nothing. In a flash I grabbed her arm and pulled her to the right, next to me. I just had time to catch Mother's terrified look It carried a wordless message: "I wonder where you are going? Perhaps I shall never see you again."

And she was gone, lost in the crowd streaming leftward. Just behind us came the little fair-haired girl with the doll, clutching her mother's hand. "*Links!*" the officer ordered casually.

And the little girl disappeared from sight, with her doll.

———✦———

Until then I had felt like a spectator rather than a victim, as if I were watching from outside, detached, while devilish things went on all around me.

Everything had to be done on the double – one-two, one-two. Dusk was falling. A weird sight in the distance caught my eye. A group of women, naked and bald, were trotting in formation out of one of the wooden huts across an empty space lit by strong searchlights. Who could they be? Where were they running to? They didn't look like human beings. More like figures from a waxworks. I was determined to stay clear-headed even if nothing made sense.

Our group that had been sent right consisted of some 300 healthy young women up to thirty-five years of age. A woman SS guard took us over and we doubled into the first wooden barracks. Inside was an empty room where we were ordered to take off all our clothes – underwear, stockings and shoes included – and leave them in a neat pile until, she assured us, we came back for them later, after we'd had a shower.

So there we all stood next to each other, stark naked. Jewellery, rings and watches were to be left with our clothes. I took everything off except the tin ring Arno had given me before he went. That, I was resolved never to be parted from. It would remain my source of strength, my hope of reunion, my torch of love. It would keep my heart warm.

We now had to go through a narrow opening in single

file to be further inspected by a uniformed SS man, to make sure we had all obeyed orders and were not trying to hide or smuggle anything.

It was nearly my turn when we heard cries and entreaties, blows and confusion. What was going on? One of the girls, it turned out, had tried to conceal an engagement ring under her tongue and the SS man had found it. She was beaten up and taken away. We had no idea where to, or what would become of her. The girl in front of me noticed I still had my ring on. "For Christ's sake take that thing off. You must be mad! He'll kill you. And just for a piece of tin that's not worth a cracker. You saw what he did to the girl in front of us!"

Only a piece of tin, as she put it. But it was all I had and I wasn't going to throw it away. It would be like betraying Arno and saying I didn't care what became of him. The ring was our bond.

I started moving backwards in the queue to give myself time to think.

Was the other girl right, or was I?

Should I throw it away or keep it?

If I throw it away, I thought, I will have deserted Arno in my own eyes and lost the moral ground under my own feet.

If I keep it, the SS man may find it, or may not. It was like Russian roulette. Perhaps my life was now at stake. My mind was made up. I decided I must keep the ring, since all my love and hope rested with it.

For better or worse, I slipped it under my tongue, just like the other girl.

I stepped in front of the SS man, knowing full well what I was doing and what risk I ran, but prepared to pay any price. I put my life on the line. He started ruffling through my hair to see what he could find. I was expecting him next to tell me to open my mouth wide.

At that moment, an order rang out from his superior to speed the inspection up. With a push he sent me on my way.

"Next one! Hurry up!"

The ring stayed with me.

It was my first test in facing up to destiny, and I had passed. The fact that I had saved the ring filled me with fresh confidence that I had nothing to be afraid of.

In the next room was a long wooden bench. About ten male guards were sitting on it, all with hair clippers in their hands. Each of us had to go up to the "barber" and have all hair shaved from her body – long or short, from the head, armpits, crotch – everywhere.

We were standing up to our knees in piles of hair. Brown, blonde, black, auburn, straight, curly. We were changed beyond recognition. My sister stood next to me, with just her eyes shining from beneath her bald scalp. We all stared at each other in amazement for a while, recognising one another only by our voices.

When the last of us had been shaved we were chased into a kind of rotunda with three tiers of benches all around going up to the ceiling. Instinct urged me to run to the very top so that I could have an overall view. The room quickly filled up with naked, shorn women, sitting motionless, packed close together, wildeyed. An eerie sight it was, like a collection of bald tailors' dummies waiting for their wigs and clothes before being arranged in a window display.

———✦———

Suddenly, a new order: "*Alle heraus!*" "All out!" We were herded into a large concrete basement "for a shower" There was a crowd of women at the door from another transport that had just joined us. Most of them were Hungarians. They insisted they had information which had never reached us in Terezín. These were not showers at all, they said, but gas sprays, and we were all going to be asphyxiated.

"Everyone inside, get on with you!" the guards shouted, and a dozen or so of them started to push us in.

The Hungarian women fought, screamed, and tried to get out, but it was useless. They were squeezed in by brute force. The steel doors were bolted behind us.

The whole ceiling was crisscrossed with a grid of metal pipes with a showerhead at each junction. Was it for water or for gas? What would be the point of spraying us with gas, I reasoned. Nonsense – we had been told we were going to have showers, and that was that. I held my sister close beside me, both of us under a showerhead.

Suddenly we felt a spray of hot water. I knew I had been right. The Hungarians had only been panicking.

There was no soap, just water. The flow stopped, the steel doors opened, and women guards moved in to drive us out again: *"Alle heraus! Schnell! Los! Heraus! Heraus!"* "Out! Out! Quick!", cracking their whips.

Wet and scalded, we emerged into the cold October night and ran on the double from one block to another across brightly-lit courtyards.

My God! Now I recognised the group of naked, hairless, waxwork women I had been so puzzled by when we arrived a few hours before. Now I knew. It was us, and all those who would come after us.

We were chased into a kind of draughty barn, lined up in fives, close together. It was not exactly my aim ever to be in the front row. I shifted to be the last in a row and as inconspicuous as possible. At that moment I became aware that nature, heedless of the situation, was asserting itself. A trickle of blood was running down my leg. How pleased I was that there was a tall girl in front of me so that the guard couldn't see me. But my luck didn't hold. The woman guard returned to inspect our row. She noticed that I was almost hidden at the far end and shouted "You there!" and pointed at me. "Move forward, quick!"

I moved up, and as soon as she saw the blood all hell broke loose.

"*Du Schwein! Du jüdische Sau!*" "Jewish pig! Filthy creature!" she screamed in a fit of rage. She pulled the whip out of her jackboot, with the lead ball at its end, bellowing like an insane thing and lashing me across the breasts.

The weapon drew blood. Now there was red everywhere. I flinched slightly, turning my head, but then stood still like a marble statue, afraid that she would kill me if I tried to fend off her blows.

At this moment a tall, thin SS woman came in and ordered her to move us into the "clothing room." That brought the guard's fit of rage to a halt and saved me. Since she had to defer to higher authority, she stuck the whip back into her boot and shouted to us to get out.

Once more we ran on the double into another barracks, a line of blood drops marking my trail. At the back of the hall were two great piles of motley clothing, no better than rags, plus another pile of assorted shoes. A guard was standing over each pile.

As we ran past, a guard threw us at random whatever she happened to pick up from the pile. And that was our clothing from then on. We had to catch it as we ran out of the barracks. Not until we got outside could I stop to look at my "presents." I found myself holding an olive-green georgette evening gown with pearls all over and flashing sequins around the deep-cut neck. Its size was indefinable – full of loose ends and trailing sleeves with more gaudy decoration.

In addition, I had been thrown a jacket to fit a twelve-year-old, blue with red stripes and a blue lining. Also a pair of socks, one short and green, the other longer and purple.

In my other hand I held a pair of men's black patent leather shoes, big enough to fit a giant.

Shivering in the cold, I quickly put everything on. The sky above was already full of stars. The piles of clothes had obviously been leftovers from the confiscated baggage of the various transports as they came. Who, I wondered, could have been the owner of the green gown I was now wearing? Why did she bring it here? What sort of place did she imagine she was going to? It had a nineteenth-century look and might have been worn in a stage play about society ladies who dressed for dinner. Well, now I would have to wear it in another sort of play with a very different setting and plot.

I threw the jacket over my shoulders and slid into the outsize shoes. Since they kept falling off I quickly squashed the backs down and flopped around in them like huge slippers, so as not to lose them. Some of the girls had been given heavy wooden clogs.

Outfitted this way, we finally reached the quarters assigned to us. It was one of the long, narrow, windowless shacks that I had seen when we arrived. There were rows and rows of them, all identical. The inside suggested a vast barn divided in half by a red brick stovepipe running up the middle of the floor. It was like a demarcation line separating left from right. I doubt whether it was ever intended to keep the shack warm. It was bitterly cold inside.

The space was filled with three tiers of bunks close together: the lowest almost on the ground, the middle one close above, the top tier only just shy of the ceiling. There were no single beds. About ten people had to squeeze together like sardines on each bunk. There was only room to sit hunched up. Since we couldn't move, we simply lay there ten to a bunk, with no cover, waiting to see what would happen next.

We immediately formed groups of similar age and interests, we girls who had known each another from Terezín. In addition to my sister Lydia, whom I now kept tight hold of, our fivesome included my old friend Marta. She had been miraculously drafted into the same transport as us with her husband, Dr Karel Bloch; Nana Krásová, wife of the composer Hans Krása, who had delighted Terezín with the children's opera *Brundibár*, and Anita Kohn, wife of the well-known oboist, Pavel Kohn. He, as we learned a few days later, had been drafted into the camp orchestra as soon as he arrived. This orchestra had to play the prisoners to work each morning, and accompany them with classical music each evening as they arrived back half-dead, or, often enough, dead.

We felt sure the five of us could help one another. If one stumbled the others would lend her moral support and keep her head above water. There would be complete mutual reliance, come what may. Those of our fellow inmates who now found themselves among total strangers were in a worse plight.

Nothing more happened that first night. We were just cold, hungry and thirsty. We were given nothing to eat or drink. In the end, worn out by the journey and by everything that had happened to us here on our first day, we simply fell asleep from exhaustion.

But before dropping off, I tore a thin strip from the lining of my jacket, threaded it through Arno's ring and hung it securely where it could not be seen under my evening gown.

I glanced down at my row of nine bedfellows, seeing them now transformed into those bald, bizarrely clad creatures I had seen behind the barbed wire fence when we arrived. Their shorn heads were like so many skulls tossed into a pile, one much like another. Where on earth had we ended up? In what unimaginably strange place?

Our outward transformation had taken no time at all. But our invisible inner strength, our moral and spiritual balance, was something we had to keep firm and inviolate, whatever twists of fate awaited us.

My thoughts went to each member of our family. Mother was no doubt in some other shed not far away. Who knows if my father and brother might not be in the same camp too, all unaware. What joy it would be to catch sight of one another, even through barbed wire!

Finally I fell asleep with the others on the hard wooden planks, in my evening theatre wear and men's patent leather shoes. And so our first night in Auschwitz passed, leaving us blissfully ignorant of the secret happenings yet to be revealed.

At five in the morning the imperious voice of the SS woman in command rang out: *"Alle heraus! Zählappell! Raus! Raus"* "All out! Roll-call! Out! Out!" as she cracked her whip in the air. We jumped down half asleep and out onto the huge parade ground. We had to form up in fives immediately. It was still dark except for a few dim stars.

The counting began: 5, 10, 15, 20 ... and so on. There were about 300 of us. After checking our numbers again the SS woman simply walked off. We had been told not to move or say a word. We stood there like soldiers on duty, silent and motionless for about three hours. When she finally returned she recounted us and shouted the next order: *"Alle ins Waschraum! Los!"* "All into the washroom! Run!"

The "washroom" was another huge barn with a concrete trough running all around the wall and a water-pipe over it with taps at one-metre intervals. Water dripped rather than flowed from them. We all rushed to the taps, pushing and shouting to get to the water. It became impossible to get near the taps. Those who were nearest drank what they could get. No one dreamt of washing. I finally managed to get my hand through the crowd under a tap and swallow a handful before the SS woman returned and ordered us on parade for yet another roll-call.

"Five, ten, fifteen, twenty ..." she shouted, then left us standing for two more hours. Still no food, and nothing to drink but the few drops I had managed to snatch in the washroom.

The sky became overcast and rain began to fall. We kept on standing there. The SS woman went off and came back in a raincoat. We had to stay soaked to the skin. If anybody caught a chill, they caught a chill. There was no avoiding it.

It was nearly midday before someone came to check the numbers once more and chase us back into our shack. We were told that two prisoners could "volunteer" to be block leaders, responsible for keeping watch over us and dividing out the bread rations. About 150 women frantically thrust up their hands, mostly Poles and Hungarians. Not a single Czech. We refrained from offering cooperation, even though we knew it would put us at the mercy of the new powers-that-be.

Finally a cauldron of soup arrived in our block, the first food we had tasted since leaving Terezín. It seemed like ten years ago rather than three days. Terezín had meanwhile disappeared from out consciousness as if it had never existed.

Our two block leaders, Hungarians, immediately started distributing the soup. One full tin between five, each of whom took it in turn to slurp it up. There were a few cabbage leaves swimming in it, which you had to fish out with your fingers. There were no spoons. It was obvious that the block leaders were keeping the biggest helpings for themselves and their friends.

We squeezed back onto our bunk, sitting like hunchbacks and wondering what the next surprise would be. In this place nothing was foreseeable.

Three male prisoners came in. One of them I instantly

recognised as Ota Weil. He had helped us with the theatre lighting in Terezín, which he had left two years ago in a transport "to the East." So now we knew where they had all been sent.

All three men were working in the camp as electricians and were able to move about freely. Ota had come to see if his sister was amongst us. I jumped down straight away to greet my old colleague. But though he recognised me he looked different now, with a strange, absent expression in his eyes like a man from another world.

"When did you get here?" he asked.

"Some time yesterday afternoon."

"Alone?"

"No, my sister's here with me. And Mother."

"Your mother's still with you, or did she go to the left?"

"Yes, she went to the left. So I suppose she's in another block with older women."

He took me to the door, opened it halfway and pointed to the column of red flames rising high up to the sky from a nearby tall chimney. "That's where she went," he remarked dryly. "She went up the chimney."

What was he babbling about? Poor Ota, he's been here two years and all the things he's seen and experienced here must have driven him crazy. I suddenly felt sorry for him and to avoid further argument said: "Yes, I suppose so."

I had seen the flames, sure enough, but persuaded myself it must be a bakery. To cope with so many mouths they no doubt had to bake bread non-stop, right through the night. Realising I was not going to see eye-to-eye with Ota, I bade him a quick farewell. I was a new arrival, still in full possession of my senses, whereas he, poor chap, was not any more.

"Everyone who went to the left was sent straight up the chimney," he added, as we said goodbye.

———✦———

Time was passing, each day like the others. We were either lying on our bunks or standing outside. Hour after hour we stood in the rain, in the mud, in puddles or wherever. If the guard was in a good mood she would hiss through her teeth "Five, ten, fifteen, twenty ..." and leave it at that. But if she had had a bad day she would cheerfully make us kneel in the mud or stand for a few hours longer.

On one occasion she announced we were going to get tattooed the next day. Everyone would get a number. Not on our forearm, as we had seen on prisoners that had been here a long time, but on our forehead.

We waited helplessly for the operation to begin, but nothing happened. A twist of fate interfered and we were never tattooed. They had run out of ink.

———✦———

Our dismal camp life dragged on. We slowly forgot the normality of existence outside: woods and nature and the setting sun; birdsong and forest murmurs; the bustle of the streets. We lost the very concept of time. The memories of home life had become a kind of odd dream.

It seemed unreal that in other places there were people sitting down to supper at this hour, whole families together, then sleeping in their own beds and each going their own way next morning. Reality was what surrounded us here in the camp. This was the only truth, the only thing that concerned us. Everything else was an illusion.

From time to time rumours circulated. Where they came from and who passed them on was a mystery. They travelled along the grapevine. We heard them all, but many made no sense to us. One report was that a lorry with a black tarpaulin cover was going around the camp and that whichever block it stopped in front of, all the inmates had to get in and were driven straight to the gas chamber. We refused to believe this, but we felt instinctively that devilish things were going on behind our backs about which we knew nothing.

Standing on the parade ground we often saw white, windowless ambulances going past with large red crosses painted on each side. If there were Red Cross vehicles around, we reasoned, they must be bringing first aid materials and medicines for the sick.

Cynics maintained that all they were delivering was gas for killing people. This we obstinately refused to believe.

One day a particularly dangerous situation confronted me.

We were chatting as usual on our bunk just under the ceiling when I saw an old Terezín friend whom I had not noticed before sitting on the other side. I decided to visit her by crawling from one top bunk to the next across the narrow gangway. Suddenly I saw an SS man standing right below. He looked up at me and bellowed: "*Runter!*" "Get down!"

I jumped down right in front of him and he eyed me carefully from head to foot.

"*Du kommst mit!*" – "You come with me!" – he ordered. As I followed him to the door I sensed that the die had been cast and there was no point resisting. I saw horror in everyone's eyes. They were convinced they were seeing the last of me.

I had no specific fears, since I had no idea what to be afraid of. Outside the block, there was no one around. We went along empty lanes between barbed-wire fences.

The guards on the lookout tower saw us and waved us by. Finally we came to a block just like ours. The officer opened the door and pushed me inside. It was completely empty, with not even a bunk in sight, just the square red brick stovepipe running along the floor from end to end. I noticed piles of objects strewn along it. I took a step closer to see better what they were. Surgical instruments.

My first idea was that he was going to kill me. I could only pray that it would be over quickly. I am completely in his power, I thought, and nothing and nobody in the world can save me. I sought comfort in fate. Consigning myself to God's hands I felt a little better. *"Ausziehen und niederlegen."* "Undress and lie down," came the command.

But the next development was not what I had been expecting. The officer simply stuck a large syringe into a vein on my arm and told me to keep pumping the blood. That was all he wanted. It flowed plentifully. I thought I might bleed to death and stopped pumping.

"Weiter machen!" "Just carry on!" he insisted, and slapped me across my face.

When he had filled all the containers he had with my blood he pricked the lobe of my ear, presumably to get a blood-group sample, and ordered me out. *"Heraus! Und schnell! Los!"* "Out with you! Quickly!"

Throwing on my evening dress and patent leather shoes I raced from the block. But now there was a new danger, for I was completely on my own. Leaving a block unaccompanied was strictly forbidden. Anyone trying to escape was shot immediately. What if the look-out sentry saw me? He would shoot me without a second thought. The best thing would be to walk slowly so as not to suggest any intention of escaping. The route along the empty paths seemed endless, and the silence was total. No sign of life anywhere. No one saw me until I finally recognised our shack and crawled inside. When the new block leader saw me she threw a fit, yelling and hitting me: "Where have you been? How dare you? We'll all be shot because of you!"

She carried on like she was demented. Coming back to the block had shaken me more than leaving it, but I climbed up quickly to the top bunk. Everybody was relieved and happy to see me back. My sister wept with joy. They wanted to know exactly where I had been and what had happened.

Even though we were sitting doubled up we were at least together, and I suddenly felt safe among these friends, almost at home. It is curious how quickly one adapts. But there was no time for long explanations. We were faced with a new situation.

The dreaded black tarpaulin lorry had stopped in front of our block. Panic arose. A dozen women guards ran in with whips in their hands, and the same number of male guards wielding truncheons. They were evidently prepared to deal with any resistance or mutiny. Forming two close ranks beside the door so that not even a mouse could escape, they commandeered us with a lot of shouting into the waiting vehicle. Those who had heard the rumours put up a violent struggle, but all in vain. With whips and truncheons they forced us all into the lorry, and then bolted it.

We could feel ourselves being driven on a zigzag route through the camp, though we could see nothing. There was chaos inside. "This is the end of us," some of the girls were wailing. "They'll gas us and we'll all be finished!"

Completely ignorant, we had no clear idea what they were talking about. Gas? Gas chambers? These were words that had hardly entered into our vocabulary. Finally the vehicle came to a stop and we jumped out. Immediately the word went around that we were standing in front of a gas chamber.

"Form fives, get counted!" We were told to stand there

until our turn came. The gas chamber was in use and we had to wait until it was empty. Why pick on our particular block? No doubt, said some, because we were unproductive and they wanted to get rid of us.

There we stood, all night and the whole of the following day, fifty-three hours with no food or water. Like people condemned to death – no further need to feed them. Thanks to a supreme effort of will, not one of us fainted.

I was not thinking of death, nor did the events of my life unfold before my eyes. I merely felt terribly thirsty after losing all that blood. I felt very tired and had a longing to sit down. But where? I summoned all my strength to stay on my feet and avoid collapsing from thirst and fatigue. But once again things were to take a quite unexpected turn.

38

Next stop eastward – Kurzbach

Suddenly the order came from on high that a transport of 2,000 women, including the thousand of us who were waiting for the gas chamber, was to be organised immediately and sent further east to dig trenches. Trenches? Where? In defence against whom? Were the Russians getting closer and were we supposed to hold them up? Our bare hands against the Soviet colossus?

Fortune had been kind to us. Strange turns of fate often occurred when least expected, even here. Instead of being consigned to the gas chamber, we were now marched off in fives to a railway track. There was already a throng of other women there. We were all squeezed into the waiting train, a passenger train this time. Soon we began to move. It seemed like a miracle that we should be leaving the horrors of Auschwitz, but the SS guards walking up and down the coaches disabused us loudly of any false hopes.

"*Ihr kommt bald alle sowieso zurück.*" "You will soon be back again," they sneered. Still, we were on our way to somewhere else, and it couldn't be as bad as here, we thought. Experience soon taught us that every change was for the worse, but it is not in human nature to accept this until it is proven to be true.

Each of us was now given a crust of bread for a three-day journey. Starving as we were, we all swallowed the whole lot immediately without a thought for the morrow. We were to be in that train, in fact, for about two days and two nights, passing through unfamiliar countryside and villages, going further and further eastward.

At last the train pulled up and we got out. This was a landscape of fields and meadows that none of us recognised.

The grapevine, however, was as busy as usual and we discovered where we were – in Upper Silesia, at a lonely spot called Kurzbach, not far from Breslau. It was already November. Along the road, the trees were leafless, the ground muddy and the sky grey with heavy clouds. A sharp breeze blew up. It started to drizzle. We were soon shivering with cold.

After a march of several hours we reached our destination. It seemed to be some kind of a farm of which only two huge wooden barns remained. One stood beside the main road, the other on a slope on the opposite side.

They assigned as many of us as possible to one or other barn; my group was put in the higher one. The remainder, some fifty women, were housed in a stable with room for ten horses. All three buildings were of thin timber with no windows. The first thousand women would stay here, we were told, and the rest would be sent further on.

The German guards in charge of us were relatively old, either demobilised servicemen or soldiers transferred to the reserve. All were in uniform with rifles over their shoulders. There were also two women guards and the camp commander, who were billeted elsewhere. They had a cabin put up for them by the roadside which served as a unit headquarters from which daily orders were issued.

When we walked into our block we found it was lined

with the familiar threetier bunks – long shelves of planks on which ten had to sleep in a row, tightly packed together. Our fivesome immediately secured a place under the ceiling, which was pretty high and left enough room for sitting up – an undreamed-of luxury.

On our arrival we were given neither food nor drink. We were soaked to the skin from the rain and freezing from the cold. Worn out, we simply fell asleep on the bare planks. We were allowed to use a latrine that had been dug for us outside the block. I ventured out. It was a dark, starless night and the rain had stopped. My wet clothes clung to my quaking limbs. When I returned to the barn it looked to me like a vast warehouse with silent human bodies laid out on the shelves – not even particularly human, more like piles of wet rags heaped up at random.

They woke us at five and immediately had us line up for the number check. Then we were split into ten squads, each given a spade, and marched to the site where we were supposed to dig trenches. We looked a bizarre lot, I in my thin green georgette evening gown with all the pearls and shiny beads on, men's patent leather shoes, bald-headed, and a spade over my shoulder.

At the place where we stopped there was nothing to be seen far and wide, only a bare, flat, treeless wilderness with no feature to rest the eye on. To find ourselves outside in the country, though, with no barbed wire in sight, did give us a slight illusion of freedom. Here, we thought, we can at least breathe fresh air. A little physical exercise won't harm us and might strengthen our muscles. There are no Auschwitz chimney flames to threaten us, and none of our ancient guards here are exactly frightening. Who knows? – our hard labour might earn us a little more food.

Anyway, the war is bound to end soon. The Russian army is near, almost at the door, so we just have to hold out for a little longer and peace will break out. There will be general rejoicing and we will all get back to our various homes. Arno will find me, as promised, whistle our theme tune and a happy new life will begin. A sudden wave of optimism rose amongst us; our mood was almost jolly.

But the smiles were soon wiped off our faces. We were faced with a new enemy now, one we found very hard to cope with. We had not yet realised that in this flat, unsheltered region of Silesia the wind can blow like an icy whip; with the wind chill, it felt like minus 25 or minus 30 degrees centigrade. Here we were, practically barefoot, close-shaven and wearing thin rags. The weather soon made itself felt.

There was still frost on the ground when we rose for roll-call at five, and we were given nothing to eat. They led us a few kilometres to the area where we were meant to dig trenches. Did they imagine a few girls, hardly able to lift a shovel, were going to put up effective barriers against the Russian army? The soil was in any case already frozen so hard that you couldn't drive a fork into it. Our spades merely rebounded idly.

We stood helplessly, not knowing what to do. True, they didn't exactly hound us or check the work done, but even standing still for ten hours in a biting wind with no food was an ordeal. We reached the work site at seven o'clock each morning. After we had stood around for two hours a little morning train would come past and whistle every day at the same spot. That meant it was nine o'clock. Our timetable for the day: eight more hours to freeze.

Limbs shaking and teeth chattering, we huddled into little knots to get some protection at least from the relentless, searing wind. At seven in the evening we shouldered our spades and marched the few kilometres back to camp, where we got a tin full of watery soup to round off the day's toil.

Twice a week we received a small piece of bread as a three-day ration. It was interesting to see the different ways human nature revealed itself. Someone had found a knife in the barn, a great treasure which we shared amongst us. One girl would cut her portion into three equal pieces, eat one right away and save the others for the next two days. Another would slit each third into thin wafers to give herself the illusion that she had five slices for supper instead of just one. One girl cut her slices into little squares, another into triangles, and both counted anxiously to see how many fragments she now had per slice. Saving up your bread exposed you to the danger of night time robbery. Yes, some were desperate enough to steal.

I had my own solution. I was hungry. Keeping and guarding the ration over three days was risky. One wretched slice wouldn't save me, nor satisfy me. So I decided I'd eat the whole three-day ration all at one go. I'd enjoy one good supper and to hell with the next two days. Those I can survive, and can at least have the pleasure of recalling one square meal. So I sat down in a corner and swallowed my bread-ration with great gusto, regretting only how hungry my friends were going to be that night, and how anxious about thieves.

December came and the winter closed in. We still had nothing to shield ourselves with from the cold, and many fell ill. We huddled close together for warmth, waiting all night for daybreak to come; then again, waiting all day to get back to the barn after standing for hours in the frost. We slept in the clothes we had on, sometimes wet through, on the bare boards, with no blankets. Our hands and feet froze during the day and water dripped into our shoes, which never dried out. We used to stand leaning on our spades with our free hands under our armpits to get a little warmth, then change hands to save our fingers from frostbite.

The unequal struggle against the cold drained our willpower as well as our energy. Morale began to sink. But we did find a way to deceive that other enemy, hunger.

39

Imaginary feasts, a needle and other wonders

The trick was to start "cooking." Merely talking about food became a substitute for food itself Our group of ten girls decided that each of us would take it in turn to prepare a splendid feast featuring at least five choice courses. The cook of the day had not only to work out the menu but to describe each course down to the last ingredient and provide recipes for every item. The scheme worked.

Banquets were served up each day that would have been a credit to any grand hotel: from the laying of the table through all kinds of soups and hors d'oeuvres, both native and foreign, followed by seafood served on scallop shells. Then, after a decent pause, the main course would arrive: meat of all kinds done in every way the cookery books had ever described. Poultry and game were accompanied by *knedliky* (Czech dumplings), potatoes, rice, noodles of all shapes and sizes and every kind and hue of vegetable, all washed down with wine. The assortment of desserts was mouth-watering. And to complete the meal, a good cup of coffee and cake with filling – topped with whipped cream, naturally.

And so we went on, turn by turn. There were some excellent cooks amongst us, vying with each other and never stinting with the ingredients.

One day there was an incident, however. The hostess

for the day was just coming to the end of her menu and explaining the recipe for a festive "Libuše cake".

"This is how we made it in our family," she said. "Blend together a pound of butter, eight dessert spoonfuls of icing sugar and ten egg yolks –" she started.

"Don't talk rubbish!" broke in a girl who had lived next door in her home town. "Your mother would never have dreamed of putting ten yolks into any kind of cake mixture. She was very tight with eggs and would have used two at the most. Ten? Never! Look, I used to come to your place and your cakes were never any good, mainly because of the eggs. Goodness knows why she was so stingy. You weren't short of a penny. So don't boast and don't tell whoppers."

The hostess of the day went red in the face and not knowing how else to defend her honour, attacked her friend physically. The two girls couldn't tear each other's hair out, as they didn't have any, so they pulled each other to the ground in a fight. We had to separate them forcibly until they calmed down. But we never found out how the recipe for "Libuše cake" ended.

We also managed to defeat the bitter cold to a certain extent. One of the in-mates in our barn was chosen as a cleaning woman for the SS woman guard in command. Instead of standing all day with a shovel, like the rest of us, she could stay in the warmth with her new employer. One night she returned to the barn with an unheard-of treasure, prized beyond gold – a needle! This needle became our salvation. We agreed that each of us should have it for one evening. And we started sewing. What did we not achieve with that one needle!

We had no proper thread, so we pulled strands out of the clothes we had on. I made a headscarf out of my jacket lining and still had enough material left over to cover my hands – lo and behold – with lace-up gloves! Now my fingers didn't freeze so badly. Each of us managed to improve her clothing somehow, especially by way of protecting the head and hands. We treasured that needle and would have given our lives for it.

By another miracle, each of us was issued a blanket around this time. Not a soft, warm, woolly one but only a thin rag of man-made fibre. Still, it was something, and we wrapped ourselves in our blankets like mummies.

One day as we walked back along the main road from work one of the local peasant women was coming our way in her warm shaggy coat and high felt boots, with a thick shawl around her head and neck and knitted woollen gloves. She had a full pack on her shoulder. When she saw us in our wretched rags with legs all raw from the frost, she stopped. She opened her pack and threw us a pair of long, thick stockings. Black, they were. I happened to be nearest to her and caught them in my free left hand. I muttered something like, "Thank you." I could have hugged her and kissed her hand. It was a wonderful present and so unexpected. We could hardly get over the shock.

When we got back to the barn each of us took turns putting them on for at least half an hour. We were a close-knit group: my sister Lydia, my good friend Marta Blochová, Nana Krásová, Anita Kohnová and myself. We decided that each of us in turn should wear the stockings for a whole day. And since it was I who had been instrumental in bringing the stockings into the gang, it was decided that I should go first. Heavy snow fell that night and all the next day. And there was I in the morning, stepping out in long woollen stockings. What comfort, what luxury! And along with my evening gown, a blue kerchief over my head now from the jacket lining, and something over my hands too, I felt fully equipped for the cold. The guards said it was 20 degrees below zero centigrade.

40

Nana's prophecies

But the winter got no milder. On the contrary, the night frosts became more intense and we had long icicles hanging from the ceiling right above our heads. As more and more of us fell sick, the camp commanders must have reasoned that we would all freeze to death unless something was done. And so we were given sleeping-bags – not the sort of soft, warm down bags with zippers that Himalayan climbers have, but ordinary paper sacks for potatoes. At least they were big and long enough to climb into. They didn't keep you very warm, but at least they were another layer to help keep frostbite away.

There was one snag about these bags, however. The stiff paper they were made of rustled and crackled loudly whenever anyone moved. The whole barn echoed with the din all night, but that was just something else to get used to. The place looked like a storeroom with bags full of goods arranged along the shelves. Nothing suggested human contents, since no heads were to be seen now.

Next to me lay Nana Krásová, a tall beauty who looked like a pale fairy, with great thoughtful eyes. At one time she had long black hair. She told me she had tuberculosis, but we still used the same spoon for eating our soup. Nana had a gift for clairvoyance. One night I woke up to see Nana sitting in her potato sack and staring into the darkness.

"Are you all right?" I asked.

"Yes, perfectly. Only I had a strange dream."

"What did you dream about?"

"I dreamed that Anita and you and I were all in Prague."

"Seems like a rather nice dream."

"Far from it. Anita and I were swimming in the Vltava River and the current pulled us away from the bank. You were standing on the Charles Bridge looking all around. You know, Zdenka," she went on, in a perfectly self-assured, matter-of-fact tone, "you're going to be the only one of us left alive. Anita and I will never return home."

Winter advanced. It was nearly Christmas time. The whole countryside lay under deep snow and digging was impossible. Perhaps they'll let us stay in the barns all day, we thought. But while in the "normal" outside world people were making Yuletide preparations, baking Christmas cakes, wrapping up confectionery and packing presents, here in our world a new ordeal awaited us. Instead of shovelling earth, the order came that we were to carry logs to a sawmill. Our dream of spending the rest of the winter in our barn melted like a snowflake in our hands.

The new project began immediately. Up at five, roll-call, then off on a long march to a distant forest, where the timber was stacked in a great pile. Each group of five women had to lift a trunk, rest it on their shoulders and march off with it. *"Marsch! Aufgehen! Los!"* "March! Keep Moving!" shouted the new guard in charge of us. We quickly spaced ourselves at equal distances under each trunk so that the load was fairly distributed. There were no proper paths in the wood and we kept falling into snowdrifts and tripping over roots.

Those who only had clogs on their feet found the snow sticking to them, their ankles continually giving way.

The logs on our shoulders got heavier and heavier, but we were not allowed to lay them down even for the occasional rest. "*Marsch!*" the cry would come from the guard on duty, who seemed forever itching to clout us with the rifle he carried on his shoulder.

At last we emerged from the forest onto the highway, where at least we were safe from tripping and could keep the log properly in place on our shoulders. As a former Sokol gymnast I saw there was only one thing to do.

"Girls," I said, "look, if we want to make it easier for ourselves we must keep in step and all march in the same rhythm. Let's sing in time." And we started up the old Czech jingle. *One – two – four horses in the yard, no one taking them to plough … trala-lalala, trala-lalala, one-two …*

Raz – dva
ctyri – kone
ve dvore
zádný – s nimi
neore
tralá – lalala
tralá – lalala
zadny s nimi
neore
raz-dva

"*Sehr gut,*" – "Very good," said the guard approvingly.

After another few kilometres we got to the sawmill. There we could drop our logs to the ground alongside the others. Our knees were knocking and we could hardly stand upright. Each of us got a small tin of thin soup for her efforts. That was our food for the day. When we returned to our barns that evening we collapsed on the bunks out of sheer exhaustion.

Our shoulders were already raw and bleeding; how long could we hold out? This was work for horses, not for half-starved girls whose health and strength were fast running out. We were covering twelve kilometres a day. Every evening we applied snow to our sores, but they were still weeping when we got up. Each day one or other of us collapsed with a high temperature and was sent to the "sick bay," a dark, grubby hole where no one looked after you. There were no drugs or medicine. You either recovered – or died.

Our condition was deteriorating rapidly. Marta was the first of our fivesome to go under. She was moved to the sick bay and we had all said goodbye to her in our hearts. But we took it in turns after work to visit her and try to keep her spirits up. "The war can't last long," we said. "Just force yourself to keep going until it's over."

Something unusual happened one day. We were walking home from work, or rather crawling, like desiccated shadows. I was last in line as usual. I always tried to be inconspicuous and never pushed myself forward to earn favour. We had had a replacement guard in charge of us that day, an older man who might have been a schoolteacher in civilian life. He walked slowly and seemed as tired as the rest of us. He carried the usual rifle but had a kind, quiet expression, as if he would rather have been sitting by his home fire in his slippers with a cat at his feet, than out here guarding prisoners.

Without warning he turned to me and said softly, "Can I give you something?" He used the polite *sie* for "you", a rare courtesy.

I couldn't imagine what he might want to give me, but not to offend him I whispered back, "Of course, surely."

Putting his hand in his pocket he drew out a beautiful white crusty roll such as none of us had seen for years. He slipped it across to me, adding apologetically, "A mouse has been at it, though."

On a closer inspection he was right. In the middle of the roll was a neatly gnawed-out crater, such as only a mouse can make. In fact the whole roll was hollow with just the crust left. Never mind, I thought, the mouse must have been hungry too. However, I was delighted to have it and could have swallowed it whole as I walked along. But suddenly I thought of Marta, ill and equally hungry in her sick bay. She was worse off than I. I must save the roll for her. A little extra can help a lot.

With a great effort I restrained myself from breaking off just a tiny bit of the crust for myself. Marta, after all, had got me off the transport in Terezín and rescued me from certain death. So I had to repay her in this small way.

As soon as we reached the barn I rushed off to find her in the sick bay and give her the biggest gift I could. She had a high temperature and was barely conscious. I told her how I had come by the roll and she really appreciated it. But the fever had made her thirsty, she said, and she would rather keep it until the morning. She took it and put it down beside her. It turned out all wrong. Someone stole it in the night, and Marta never got any of it.

I was still touched by the guard's kindness. Not every German in charge was a beast and sadist, it seemed. There were decent people amongst them who had been caught up in the maelstrom of war against their will, and could find no way out. We never saw him again. I often thought of him.

Back in the barn I lay down to sleep, little knowing what surprises awaited me that evening. I had Nana Krásová on my left and my sister on my right, where I could keep a constant eye on her. We had said goodnight when Lydia suddenly sat up. "There's something I must tell you," she said.

"Couldn't it wait till tomorrow?" I suggested, thinking it would be something trivial like a complaint about one of the other girls.

"No, I must tell you now."

"Very well, then," I agreed casually, not considering it of much importance. Then it dropped like a bombshell.

"I'm pregnant". Silence.

I gasped, "You? Pregnant? For Christ's sake, this is all we need now! How on earth did it happen?" She was just sixteen-and-a-half.

"Do you remember," she faltered, "those two transports of young men who left Terezín in September? Our brother Jirka was in one of them and my friend Petr in the other. Petr and I were very fond of each other and wanted to have a proper farewell. A mate of his lent us his attic room and that's where it happened. It was my first time. We promised we'd get together again after the war. And the next day Petr was gone."

"Not possible! This is disastrous! Pregnant, in this place? With no proper food? And hard labour? And no medical help? How is this going to end up?"

"I don't know. Perhaps the war will be over soon."

"If it started in September, and now it's December, that means you're three months gone. So you might give birth in June? Supposing someone notices before then? You remember in Auschwitz how all the pregnant women were sent to the left? God knows what became of them. The main thing now is to keep it absolutely secret. Not a living soul must know except us two. God almighty! How am I going to protect you now?"

It was a nightmare. I started watching Lydia closely. I was six years older. She was thin as a rake, but her belly was already bulging a little. Our rations were so meagre that the few spoonfuls I could spare of my own soup helped a little. A worse problem was the strain of manhandling those tree trunks over several kilometres into the mill each day. To make it easier for her, I took up the end position with her just in front of me. The timber hardly touched her and the main weight fell on my shoulder. I could only pray that no one would notice her condition.

Time moved on inexorably. It was now the beginning of January 1945, and still there was no change on the horizon.

One night Nana Krásová suddenly sat up in bed again, woke me up, and said with a serene smile, "You can't imagine what a lovely dream I've had."

"About Prague again?"

"No. This time I dreamed I was standing in the middle of a lovely green meadow, when up trotted a group of white horses, twenty-one of them. My Hans was sitting on one. He smiled and motioned to me to get into the saddle with him. I climbed up and we rode off together into the distance. He told me that where we were going there would be plenty of everything."

"Do you think this dream means anything for the future?"

"Yes. But nothing good. Not yet."

"Why? It was a beautiful dream."

"Zdenka," she said in her prophetic style, "we will see big changes on the twenty-first of this month. Changes for the worse."

And she just stopped talking about it.

41

The death march

I had some confidence in Nana's predictions and in the back
of my mind was curious to see what would happen on the
twenty-first. But nothing happened at all; it was a day like
any other. Roll-call at five, march to the woods, haul logs to
the sawmill. We didn't even feel like singing on the march,
since that used up energy too. We gulped down our tins of
thin soup and slogged it back to the barn, looking forward
to crashing down on our plank bunks, crawling into our
paper sacks and shutting our eyes. Then we could forget
the cold and hunger and thank God for letting us survive
another day.

But it was not to be like that at all.

Having been counted several times over at evening
parade we were just expecting to be released when the
Lagerkommandant, whom we had rarely seen, appeared
before us with official orders.

"Kurzbach has to be evacuated. Those in the sick bay
will stay behind, the rest of you will line up here and march
off this evening. In one hour's time."

Nana was right. The worst was still to come. So far we
had seen and experienced nothing. We went back to our
barns, but had nothing to pack for our next journey. I did
stuff a little straw into my men's shoes for fear that they

would fall off. God alone knew where we would have to march to, and how long it would take.

Suddenly Blanka Krausová, a strong, courageous girl who was a distant relation of mine from Prague, came bounding in and shouted breathlessly, "Girls, there's a cellar full of potatoes around the corner. Hurry up and get yourselves some for the journey!"

There were indeed potatoes galore. Each of us took as many as she could and stuffed them wherever we could find room – into our sleeves or under our clothes, tying string below them so that they shouldn't drop out. These potatoes were our only luggage.

Then there was Marta in the sick bay. Had the Lagerkommandant not said that all the sick cases would be left behind? Why? What would happen to them? Feverish debate ensued, but there was no time to waste. We decided unanimously not to leave Marta behind in the camp.

We ran to the sick bay and dragged her out, fever and all. She had heard nothing. No one had told those inside that the camp was being evacuated. She could hardly stand, but we managed to persuade her it was out of the question to stay, and that she must summon her last reserves of strength and march off with us. We were given a final three-day bread ration made with some kind of bran, all black and mouldy. But if you are hungry you can eat anything.

We set off, marching in fives through the frosty night. We were accompanied by an unusual number of uniformed German guards with rifles. We had not gone far before we heard violent shouts and screams from the women still locked up in the sick bay, followed by rifle shots.

They had shot every single patient.

A deathly silence spread through the countryside.

The Russian army had come closer now and was advancing rapidly westward. The Germans were determined that we, as their prisoners and witnesses to Nazi atrocities, should not fall into Russian hands at any price. So they were hounding us back west, deep into German territory. We had landed in a sector of the war front and could hear gunfire and explosions echoing day and night. It was music to our ears, for we were confident the Russians would move faster than us and would catch up with us any day now, perhaps any hour.

We had to keep marching on. Day and night, night and day.

We were overtaken on the road by lorries crammed high with migrating humanity as the villages in the area were evacuated. People were leaving their homes in haste, often bringing their cattle and poultry with them. The roads were congested with vans and covered wagons. Everyone was in flight, taking whatever he could manage in the hope of saving his life at least. In the general haste whole towns were soon on the move with the mighty Russian army at their heels.

For three days we had neither food nor sleep. The pilgrimage was becoming a gruesome Calvary. We envied the refugees the canvas cover on their wagons that protected them from the wind and snow, and their ability at least to sit up straight or even lie down.

The potatoes we had stocked up with began to weigh us down like stones. Now and again we ate one raw for the juice and starch, and it even staved off some of our hunger. There was a Prague milliner, Mitzi Poláčková, in the row behind me. She had not taken any potatoes with her. Now she tapped me on the shoulder and said apologetically:

"Zdenka, excuse me. Do you think you could lend me a few potatoes? I'll return them to you after the war." I gave her what I could spare. Goodness knows whether they were of any help. In the end they became a heavy burden we had to get rid of. With heavy hearts we dropped them along the road.

Lack of sleep was a far worse problem. We were at the point of collapse after three days and nights of continuous movement with the temperature falling well below what we thought we could endure. Breathing was difficult and our noses were transformed into frozen white icicles.

Our very despair produced an idea that saved us. We discovered it was possible to sleep on the march. Nature is merciful. Whoever's turn it was to take a nap would move to the middle of our fivesome, so that those on each side could take her arms and steer her. Sensing this support, the one in the centre could nod off, while her legs were moving automatically. She could sleep for at least two hours like this and get over the deadly exhaustion for a while. We all took it in turns to benefit from this brainwave.

Nevertheless, our ranks were starting to thin out. The weaker ones could not keep pace and gradually fell back, which was fatal. Anyone who got out of line and fell exhausted in the snow by the wayside was shot without mercy by the nearest German. No power on earth could stop the murderous finger on the trigger. Many girls who had been given heavy clogs that slowed them down took them off and marched barefoot in the snow, simply to stay in line and avoid a bullet from the nearest rifle. But by the fifth day not even the greatest willpower could stand up to the hunger, cold and exhaustion. Women and girls everywhere were dropping into the deep snow to find a peaceful, white grave.

Confirming my worst fears, Lydia now began to fail too. She had been dragging herself along like a ghost, hardly able to put one foot in front of another. Hanging on to my shoulder she whispered, "I can't go on any more. I'll have to stay here. Leave me here. You go on."

I could see she could walk no further. But what now,

for God's sake? Was I to leave my sister here, just like that? Just say goodbye and wait to hear the rifle shot, and then silence? And march on with the others, not even looking back?

Is death so simple, a light and silent thing like the snowflakes falling around us? Or should I break rank too, stay with her and be shot as well? No. That I could not allow. Neither solution was acceptable. Lydia would have to muster her reserves and march on. Both of us must survive.

Everything inside me was in revolt.

Somewhere within each of us there is a survival kit. We never know where it is, or what is in it, until it opens at the critical moment. It contains no drugs or bandages, just firm instructions about what to do – and the necessary strength to do it. That immense, mysterious strength that we never knew we possessed wells up from hidden depths, but only in extreme situations when our lives are at stake. We don't understand where it comes from, or by what miracle it helps us to achieve the impossible.

After I had talked tough to Lydia, and virtually ordered her to go on walking, she managed to pull herself together. We put her into the centre of our fivesome so that she could sleep for a while and get over the worst of her fatigue.

At last they found us somewhere to stop for the night. It was a locked barn with straw piled up in several layers. Inside, it was pitch dark and we couldn't see a millimetre in front of our noses. When they had shoved us all in they locked the door again. There was complete chaos. Pandemonium broke out. There was no room for the hundreds of us to get any sleep. We had to lie across each other, and got up in the morning as tired as if we had fought a pitched battle.

Wherever we stopped after that we came to realise that the best place to sleep was with the cattle. There was always a fight for places in the cowshed. It was luxury to lie there on dirty straw with the smell of milk and animal warmth all around. There was even some light, and if you managed to grab a spot you could stretch your bruised and weary limbs out. Spending a night with animals, I found out, was not the worst thing in the world. It was less risky, in fact, than with people. So we spent the night among horses, cows, goats and sheep.

Our numbers, alas, were diminishing. More and more girls ended up in the snowdrifts, their corpses lining the route we had taken.

It must have been the tenth day when we got to the bank of the Oder River, in late January. It was flowing fast and furious, with high waves and ice-floes in between.

As our column came to a halt the Lagerkommandant suddenly appeared and delivered himself of the mystifying command:

"*Wer kann – wetter; wer nicht – bleiben.*"

We turned the words of this Delphic oracle around in every direction, and finally decided that it meant, "Whoever has the strength should keep going; whoever hasn't, stays put."

But he never explained. What did "keep going" mean? Where to? For how much further? And what then? And what did "staying put" imply? The Russians were bound to arrive in a day or two. Would the Germans hand us over to them alive, or shoot us all first as they had shot the stragglers on the march?

Marta, for all her heroic efforts to get this far, was the first of us to decide to stay put. She just could not manage any more. Many other girls reached the same conclusion. Others weighed the alternatives. Was it better to stay, not knowing whether the Germans would let us be taken alive, or to go on? After about seventy girls had opted to stay I was still undecided.

The Kommandant had said that those who could, should carry on. I for one still had the strength to carry on, and to drag Lydia with me. At a time like this everyone had to make their own choice, knowing best where their own strength lay.

There was no bridge or ferry across the huge river, only open rafts. They loaded as many of us on as the rafts would take without sinking. We were still a big group and stood awash up to our knees in icy water. There was nothing to hold on to and with the strong current the rafts tossed us violently from side to side. Scared that we might all drown, we held on frantically to each other. After tossing crazily between waves and ice floes we finally reached dry ground on the other side, and discovered that only about half of us had survived the journey from Kurzbach. Marta was the first of our fivesome to go missing. What had happened to her after our departure we didn't know.

42

Gross Rosen camp

We marched on for another four days and felt as if we had crossed half the European continent in the last two weeks. In fact, we had covered nearly 450 kilometres, all in rags and virtually without shoes.

Finally we arrived at the gate of Gross Rosen concentration camp. The six hundred of us who were left from the original thousand felt glad to have arrived anywhere at all. It hardly mattered that we were behind barbed wire again. How did the saying go? "Times change, and we change with them." My first impressions were not that bad. There was a bit of nature to be seen, with forest all around, and trees always have a relaxing effect. We almost felt safe. The roof over our heads protected us from severe frost, and we no longer had to march anywhere. The authorities did not have their eyes on us here, and we had no duties to carry out. We went for our soup twice a day and otherwise lounged about on the floor, where we also slept. There was, of course, a roll-call twice a day to check our numbers.

Gross Rosen was mainly a camp for men. Columns of prisoners went past us every day on their way to the mines, but they were hardly human. In their long striped coats and convict caps they looked like shadows of men from whom the last drop of life had been squeezed. Their expressionless eyes gazed at us absentmindedly, as if they no longer quite belonged to this world.

Alive, but dead. Dead, but alive.

Night fell over our new camp. Everything sank into a deep silence, and we relapsed into restless sleep. I sneaked out of the hut, surrounded by dense barbed wire and the silent, clear, frosty night. There was no one around, only the stars winking down at the human race. No, not winking – rather, mocking the follies, vanity and pettiness of its transitory, short-lived presence on the planet. They seemed to be saying how trivial and ridiculous man was, with his wars and pride in his silly little victories. Men's lives last no longer than a mayfly's, and they have no idea how to spend them. Gaze upon us, say the stars, we alone are eternal!

43

Onward to Mauthausen

We had been at Gross Rosen barely a week, and hardly warmed ourselves up, when reports suddenly circulated that Russian units were near and the camp was to be evacuated. Its entire population was to set forth again, deep into western Germany, tens of thousands at a time.

With our memories of the last journey, its horrors and privations, we were more than anxious. But this time a long railway train was awaiting us. We were delighted that fortune had granted us this tiny piece of luck, never mind that it was a goods train with low, open coal trucks. At least we were going for a ride, we told ourselves, instead of having to go on foot. But once again it proved that every change was a change for the worse. This time, it was far worse than we could imagine. It was another step closer to death and annihilation for all of us.

We arrived at the siding where the train stood. They told us to climb up quickly and stand in the trucks. There were about ninety of us squeezed side by side in each truck. We thought there was no more room for a mouse, let alone a human body. How wrong we were.

Another group of women waiting on the station platform were now told to join us. Another forty bodies were jammed into each truck. But there is a limit to everything; as it was, each of us was standing on one leg, 130 of us packed so tightly we could hardly breathe. Instinct warned me to hold tight to the waist-high rim on the side of the truck and not to let go on any account. There lies your salvation, I told myself. Getting squashed among the mass of bodies in the middle would be fatal.

The train moved off and hysterical cries for help came from those huddled in the centre. They could neither stand nor breathe.

For a day and a night the train drove on through empty German villages. Nowhere was there a sign of life. We stopped at no stations and were given neither food nor drink. We were so desperately thirsty that when a little snow fell it seemed like manna from heaven. We frantically licked up every flake, wherever it had fallen. In our enthusiasm we hardly noticed that the snow had turned to rain, and in ten minutes we were drenched. With nothing to protect us, our clothes soaked up the water and froze us to the marrow. Shivering in the cold night air and with eyelids drooping from fatigue, we longed for sleep. It was already our third day in the train.

We were tossed from side to side like passengers in a storm-tossed ship, with no room to shift from one leg to the other. Those who no longer had the strength to stand collapsed onto the floor of the truck, where the mixture of coal-dust and excrement had turned into a sticky, foul-smelling slime. At the first jolt of the train the rest then fell on top of them like an avalanche, trampling some of them to death. We had no choice; no one could help himself, let alone the others. Desperate shouts for help echoed through the empty countryside as our trainload of half-crazed passengers hurtled along.

Every minute another bout of panic arose, and more fatalities followed. I lost my balance at one point, when the others pushed me. Somebody's corpse lay below me. Unable to get back on to my feet, even onto one leg, I spent the night sitting on it. The only place where I could put my hand to prop myself up was on the teeth of the corpse's open mouth.

After five days of this hellish journey we came to a halt on a siding where a sign read WEIMAR. Station staff came and opened the sides of the trucks. Within a few minutes the whole platform was transformed into a huge scrap heap, with corpses piled high in front of each truck, tossed out like so much useless human rubbish. And this in Goethe's Weimar, once the symbol of German culture and a high point of civilisation. And those who remained in the trucks? We were happy to have more room. The human will to survive is indomitable – and callous.

But our journey had not finished. We were to be transferred to a train bound for Buchenwald. But at the last moment they discovered Buchenwald was full. So we were to carry on to another place we had never heard of: Mauthausen.

We were half dead anyway and quite indifferent to where we were going next. Another three unbearable days followed, with the usual cold, hunger, thirst and death. At last they did give us something to eat: mouldy bread and some sort of cheese. But our mouths were too dry to swallow a bite; we had no saliva left.

The journey went on endlessly and we believed it would never stop. But stop it did, late on one cold evening in mid-February. It was a little hillside station bearing the simple sign: MAUTHAUSEN.

We were not even clear what part of Europe we were in. Someone thought it was Austria. If so, we had come quite a way. But why the Germans at this juncture should be pushing us around from one place to another, sometimes by train, sometimes on foot, no one could explain. All we could see was that there were fewer of us each day.

We crawled out of the trucks as fast as we could manage – everything had to be done for the Germans on the double, one-two. We found our limbs had turned as stiff as logs from the journey and gave way as soon as we tried to walk upright. Many of us had lost our shoes in the train and were now trying to trudge barefoot through the mud and snow.

Slowly we could make out, high up on the hill, the thick walls that surrounded the fortress of Mauthausen. White stone walls gleamed ominously through the darkness. With the last of our energy we clambered up the endless hill. With Marta gone, the four of us still held together. I had held my sister Lydia close beside me in the train, while Nana and Anita were on the other side. We had been able to see each other over the heads of the rest, but there had been no means of contact through the mass of bodies in between.

Now, however, we were together again at the entrance to this fortress. We passed through the great grey stone gate. Our first impression was of meticulous tidiness – and the silence, a frightening, total silence. The air seemed thick with it. Not a sound could be heard. It was as if the whole camp had some hideous, closely-guarded secret to hide. A vague oppression gripped us. Our nerves, always on edge, told us to expect cold steel at our throats at any moment.

We were led into a long, dark, narrow passageway clad on both sides with huge granite squares.

Someone suddenly seized my neck from behind. I was always last in line and twisted my head around close to one of the stones.

"Have a good look!" he said with a devilish grin. "Each stone, one head!" It was the SS guard accompanying our column.

Just what did he mean, "Each stone, one head?" We outsiders had no inkling of what went on here. But a few days later we found our explanation.

———✦———

Mauthausen was a men's camp. We were the first female transport to be sent there. In addition to the large Jewish contingent, the inmates were mostly political prisoners of all nationalities.

Deep down, all around the fortress, were great granite quarries where the prisoners worked. The rocks were first split with dynamite. Then the prisoners had to haul the heavy lumps on their backs up about 180 steps to the workplace. It was a favourite sport of the guards, when a prisoner had reached the topmost step with his last gasp, to give him a kick so that he and his load hurtled down into the depths together. Thousands of prisoners had perished here over the last few years. Now we knew what it meant: one head to each stone.

We were immediately ordered to the showers and the usual speculation began. Water or gas? We were past arguing. Water, it had to be water, water, water. We were so parched with thirst. There is nothing more unbearable – far worse than cold or hunger. There is no antidote for thirst. Cold can be overcome by movement for a while, and even hunger can be tricked. But thirst is sheer torture and only water restores life.

They turned on the showers. Hot, rusty-coloured water came down on us. We all stood underneath with mouths wide open, like fish gasping for air. No one thought of washing. We just drank and drank. Saved at last. Then we threw on our dirty, torn rags and ran across the concrete parade ground. They herded us into a brick building and locked the door.

Inside, the rooms were lined with the usual three-tier bunks, packed side by side. There were a lot of us, and very little room. Somehow we had to fit in. Four girls, they said, had to sleep on each tier. Four on each narrow shelf? This, with the best will in the world, seemed impossible. But experience had taught us that nothing was impossible in these places. Two SS women guards with whips burst in and started lashing around at random. "Get onto your beds. Quickly now!"

Each of us squatted in one corner of a tier, legs folded underneath. Twelve to a bunk, like monkeys in a cage. This won't do for long, we thought.

But our foursome soon hit on a practical solution.

"Girls, if we're going to get any sleep," I said, "and stretch our legs a bit so that they don't get paralysed, let's try this idea. Two of us on each tier can stretch out until midnight, while the other two stay doubled up. Then after midnight we'll swap over. That way we'll all get some rest. How about it?"

Everyone agreed. We took our places, and the rest of the room, seeing what we had done, did the same.

There was no work here for us to do. It was evidently just a place to stay. Rations consisted once more of a tin of thin soup a day and a piece of mouldy grey bread. Twice a day we went on roll-call to be counted. For the rest of the time we were locked up in our building, speaking to no one else and seeing no one else.

We had been there nearly a week when the rumour spread that we were going to be sent on somewhere yet again. We felt like eternal pilgrims. We were anticipating the next stage in our journey with horror. Judging by the last, we were not likely to survive it. It was still February, and in our pitiful rags we seemed doomed to freeze to death.

44

The SS man with his revolver

Something unexpected happened that night. I had been woken by the sudden glare of a searchlight illuminating the entire parade ground beneath our window.

I crawled down from my bunk and stood beside the window to see what was going on. For a moment there was silence. No one in sight. Then I saw two prisoners crossing the parade ground diagonally, carrying a wooden stretcher piled high with clothes. They walked quite normally, not at the usual trot. When they were about halfway across an SS man appeared with a revolver in his hand, obviously keeping an eye on them. I went on watching. The operation kept recurring. But I noticed that the SS man didn't turn up every time. Most times he was there, other times he wasn't.

It was then that a crazy idea occurred to me. Sometimes, in extreme desperation, we do something so at odds with our normal judgement that it borders on madness.

If we were not to freeze to death on the next stage of our journey, I reasoned, we had to get hold of some more clothes by hook or by crook. And right now I could see clothes in abundance passing just underneath our window. A wild notion got hold of me. Why not jump out of the window and nab a supply off the stretcher? The prisoners wouldn't harm me. But what about the SS man who followed them?

One time yes, then sometimes no. It would be like Russian roulette. My mind was made up. If my luck was out, he would shoot me dead. If it was in, we would all be warmly dressed for the journey.

Something clicked in my head. No second thoughts – now do it! I opened the window, jumped out just as the stretcher was passing and ran after it across the parade ground with the searchlights beaming from all corners. Springing between the two prisoners, I grabbed an armful of the clothes and rushed back. They were startled and stopped in their tracks. There was no SS man coming, though I hardly looked to see. Throwing the things up through the window – we were on the first floor – I climbed the wall like a wildcat, shot through the window and closed it behind me. In normal circumstances I would never have managed it, but when our lives are in the balance we are capable of working miracles.

Still catching my breath, I turned around and squinted through the side of the window to see what ensued. The next two prisoners were just arriving with their stretcher load of clothes. The SS man was following about ten paces behind them with his revolver at the ready. He twirled it around his forefinger as he went.

45

Nana's end, and the journey across Czech territory

Only two days after that adventure an SS woman told us we were being dispatched on our next lap the same day, so it was all out on the parade ground to be counted.

We stood as usual in groups of five. After losing Marta we had drafted Blanka Krausová into our group, the girl who had found us the cellar full of potatoes in Kurzbach. We were a good team.

Nana Krásová was in the centre position. It was a gorgeous, sunny winter's day, when in other, long forgotten times, the snow would have squeaked merrily under our feet in warm snow boots and the blue sky would have smiled down upon us on some Austrian mountainside.

Suddenly it all happened.

The SS women had just checked our numbers and were leisurely marching to and fro in front of us, when suddenly, without warning, Nana stepped out of her rank and walked off slowly in no particular direction, as much as to say, "I'm finished with all this. This is not for me any more. I'm leaving. You have a good time."

We all froze in astonishment. Even the SS women stared in disbelief. They had never seen anything like it. It was just inconceivable to them that anyone should break ranks and step out of the line.

As calm as could be, like a sleepwalker, Nana went up to the wire fence separating us from the rest of the camp. As she leaned on the wire with her back, her face to the sun, a smile flitted across her features. Perhaps she was imagining her Hans coming on his white horse to take her "where there was plenty of everything", as she had once described her dream to me in Kurzbach. Then quietly she slipped to the ground and died on the spot. It was a sheer act of will. The wire was not electrified.

We stood rooted to the ground. The SS women sprung into action at last. They ran to the wire fence and dragged Nana by her feet off the parade ground.

Shortly afterwards we were lined up and marched downhill from the fortress to the little station where we had arrived in our decimated state just a few days before.

There was a train already waiting for us. Neither a cattle train nor a coal train, but a regular passenger train with coaches marked FIRST CLASS and SECOND CLASS, with large clean windows that could be pulled down. Obviously some mistake, we reasoned. "This must be meant for some of the local bigwigs, camp commanders or whatever. They'd never let us onto a posh train like this. Better be prepared for a longish wait till they find the right rolling stock for us."

But we were wrong; it really was our train. It was unbelievable. We began to speculate that there had been a major mix-up which would have some disastrous consequences. But no. It was our train, all right, and we finally got on it. There were plenty of seats for us all, especially now that there were so few of us still alive. Destination unspecified, as usual. As we moved off we really felt that this time things were going to be better. How indomitable human nature is!

For a while we continued through unknown territory, unsure even of our direction. But then we started seeing signs and station names that told us beyond all doubt we were in the German-occupied Protectorate of Bohemia-Moravia.

"Girls, we're back home!" the cry went up, and those of us in the coach who were Czech broke into the national anthem "*Kde Domov Muj?*" – "Where Is My Home?"

"The war might end while we're on this train, and then we can go straight to our homes," we thought.

Pulling open the windows, we started shouting to people on the roads and station platforms that we were Czech. But no one answered, or waved to us or gave us anything.

There was no one in charge of us, no SS guard coming through the coaches, no one to give us orders. We felt very cheerful, and started singing Czech folk songs. It was like a school outing on Czech soil. Looking out of the window now I saw a well-known landscape, the beloved features of my home region. Everything, including the view from the window, suddenly fell into place in the mosaic of this latest illusion. *I am back home! Back in my home town!*

As if in collusion, the train slowed down just short of our station and then halted for a few minutes. After everything, back in Rokycany! I felt like saying to my sister: "Look here, Lydia, why don't we simply get out and walk straight home. We'd slip out of these rags, get into a long, hot bath, use our own soap, toothpaste and toothbrush that we haven't seen for years, and get into fresh warm clothes, stockings and proper shoes. Then we could wait for the rest of the family to get back. Father and Mother, Jirka, my Arno and your Petr."

Just for a moment it seemed a simple, sensible possibility.

Of course I thought that the train must be locked so, "I must leave a message somehow that I was here." I got a piece of paper and a pen and wrote a note. "Here I am in the train on the station. We don't know where we are going, but we will all meet again at home. Best regards to Rokycany. From Zdenka Fantlová." I folded it into a little square and wrote on it the name Alfred Fischer, who was an employee of my father. And I threw it down onto the platform into the mud and slush and snow and forgot all about it.

At that point the train jerked and we were on our way again. My dream about walking back home had evaporated like a mist.

Fifty years later, when I went back to my hometown somebody said: "There is a message Mr Fischer's family has, and would you like to see it?" It was my little note that I had thrown onto the platform all those years before. They had kept it. When I saw it again it felt very, very weird. It was as if an unknown hand had touched me, and the people around me got gooseflesh. I thought what should I do with it? And I decided it belonged to this town Rokycany. The museum mounted it on a big sheet with an inscription, and the little note is there on display in the museum to this day.

Soon we pulled into Plzen station. The train came to rest on a siding behind the Skoda munitions works. Some workers ran up to the wire perimeter. We shouted to them that we were Czech. Had they got any bread?

Someone immediately produced a couple of long loaves and threw them over the fence. The others shouted encouragement. "Make a dash for it! Run away! Don't worry, we'll hide you!"

I couldn't resist. At the sight of the bread they'd thrown us I jumped out of the train, oblivious to whether a guard would shoot me or not. I grabbed the bread in my arms and rushed back onto the train.

It was so long since we had seen anything like it – lovely fragrant bread, freshly baked to a light brown and dusted with flour underneath. We shouted our thanks from the window. They waved to us and wished us a safe journey.

What a feast we had in the compartment! We divided it all equally and took slow bites from it with our eyes shut. Each piece was solemnly swallowed like the holiest of sacraments. And we never noticed that we had crossed the frontier of the Protectorate and were back on German soil.

Here it all looked very grim and uninviting, and our optimism and high spirits began to seep away. To cheer ourselves up we began telling each other the first thing we would do when we returned home.

Anita's husband, Pavel, was the oboist in the Auschwitz orchestra and she had had no word from since those days. Her contribution now was: "I shall stay at home till Pavel appears in the doorway, throw myself around his neck – and then we'll go off to the pastry shop together and eat everything they've got on the counter."

Blanka Krausová had different ideas. "As soon as I get back to our place in Prague I'll nip across the street to the pork butcher's, buy a whole bag of hot dogs and bring them home for the family. We'll gorge ourselves on them, with mustard and salt rolls. Everyone will be allowed to eat as many as he can manage. That'll be a feast and a half!"

Lydia was already five months gone and couldn't wait for the war to be over. She was as thin as the rest of us, and though her figure was starting to show her condition, her loose clothes disguised it. She and I were the only ones who knew.

It was the fourth day of our latest journey. We took it in turns to sleep in the luggage nets, which were easy to get up into. We were now in a region subject to air attacks aimed at Dresden. Incendiary bombs were flying here, whistling through the air with a *wheeeh! boom!* and lighting up the sky more and more frequently.

We didn't even care if we were hit. Every bomb that went off near us was greeted with a round of applause.

46

Bergen-Belsen

At last, at midday on the fifth day, the train came to a halt for good. The rails went no further and we all got out. By now we could hardly recognise one another. Unwashed and emaciated, with sunken cheeks and weary eyes, we had the fatalistic look of people who counted on no more miracles to rescue them.

It was a wintry, late-February day. The sun shone but gave little warmth. All around us stretched a flat, silent plain where only birch trees grew. There was still a layer of powdery snow everywhere, a scene that had always delighted us as children. The birches stood to attention and lent a silent, peaceful air to the landscape. There was a sign beside the track that read BELSEN, with an arrow pointing left.

I took a deep breath of the clean, cold air and thought: How beautiful it is here. Nothing nasty can happen to us in such lovely, quiet countryside. We had yet to learn that Belsen would prove the worst of all the concentration camps. If the others were the antechambers of hell, Belsen was hell itself.

Finally we entered the camp and saw row after row of low, windowless wooden huts among the trees. At first sight it suggested a quiet holiday camp in a birch glade. They led us on and on, almost to the furthest row, where they drove about 250 of us into one hut. There were the usual three-tier bunks, on top of each other, each for twelve people. So once more it was four to a wooden plank.

At this time, we discovered, the whole place was already crowded with thousands upon thousands of prisoners from all the camps that had been liquidated in the eastern territories. Some had arrived by train, some had had to march here. Only the toughest had made it.

As soon as we arrived each of us was faced with a battle for food: thin soup and a tiny ration of bread. It was everyone for himself here. Anyone who expected to find some semblance of order soon learned how useless it was to appeal for reason and patience in Polish, Hungarian or any other language. "Quiet! ... Don't fight! ... Be reasonable! ... Everyone should get some!"

People were scrambling for food like wild animals. Grabbing at mess tins, they took the container with the soup by the handle. In the chaos it overturned and half the soup spilled on the floor. The rest was all gone in a minute. Only those who had fought ruthlessly for it got something. The rest, including those who had tried to keep order, were left hungry. It reached the point where we prayed for German guards to be put in charge, for only they were capable of imposing discipline.

The next day we were shifted to a "labour block". There was no difference: still the same three-tier bunks with twelve huddled together like a human skyscraper. Those on the bottom tier, almost at floor level, had no room to sit up, those in the middle squashed in between, and those on the top tier touched the ceiling.

Our surviving foursome, my sister Lydia, Anita, Blanka and I, used the same system we had hit upon in Mauthausen. Two of us squeezed back at the end so that the other pair could stretch their legs and get a little sleep up until midnight. Then we swapped over so that the first two had a chance. But despite our best efforts, we didn't get any rest in our uncomfortable, twisted positions.

The daily routine was the same here as elsewhere. Awake at five, roll-call outside in fives for counting, standing and waiting ... standing ... waiting ... whatever the weather, sick or well.

Then we were marched off for "work", though there was no work to do. The SS women simply led us in formation out into the fields somewhere. There we stood all day until returning to the camp in the evening. For this effort we were supposed to get an extra ration of soup, but didn't. Bread was promised, but never came. We were all starving. I feared for Lydia now. How was she going to carry on in this place? Supposing the war didn't end, and she had her child here?

One day in the course of our "work" we came across a barrel full of rubbish and stinking bones, with a little greenish meat and yellow fat still clinging to them. We pulled them out and started gnawing at them like famished animals. No thought of food poisoning occurred to us. It was simply a feast. We swallowed the stuff with relish and left a pile of bones licked clean. When we were moved to another work site after a few days we cherished fond memories of that barrel of bones with green meat.

A day later, on our way back to camp, I spotted something shining in the mud. After picking it up and cleaning it a little I saw that it was a heavy silver dinner knife. The broadest part of the handle was engraved with a swastika. Evidently it had belonged to the SS officers' mess. They ate off silver. That'll come in handy, I thought, and hid it down my violet-coloured sock. It was longer than the green one, which only covered my ankle.

And did it get used! Not just for grubbing up roots in the fields, or cutting up the odd discarded raw potato; all sorts of things were to be found in the bins outside the SS mess that could be cleaned, sliced and eaten. I claimed that piece of cutlery for myself and took great care of it. The knife and Arno's tin ring, which hung around my waist and sustained my hopes of reunion, were the two things that kept me going.

One day, however, we had an unscheduled body check as we came back to camp. It was conducted by Irma Grese, the blonde commander of the women's section of the camp and the most sadistic of our guards. She immediately found the knife on me, pulled it out of my sock and started screaming:

"*Du jüdisches Dieb! Du Sau! Du elendes Schwein!*" "You Jewish thief! You dirty pig!" Still carrying on like a madwoman, she bashed me with the handle until I thought she would crack my skull. Then she gave me a kick and threw the knife away furiously into the mud. The fivesome following us moved up, but I knew I was not going to leave the knife behind. I had to get it back at any price. In the confusion around me I crawled against the stream to get nearer to it. Blanka grabbed me by the arm.

"You're mad," she said. "If Grese catches you with that knife again she'll have you shot on the spot! Let it be, for God's sake. Forget the bloody knife! It isn't worth it."

She was no doubt right, but I wasn't listening. I edged back through the crush, stretched an arm out into the mud … and the knife was mine. Grese didn't see me and I had what I wanted.

Determination, courage and good luck. Those are life's main essentials.

Time went on. It was already March 1945. The snow thawed and turned into a sticky yellow mud. Nothing changed from one day to the next, as if no war was in progress. We had our routine, and the outside world disappeared and became irrelevant. We could no longer imagine people elsewhere living differently from ourselves. We were getting weaker. The catastrophic lack of nourishment showed; we declined steadily in strength, weight and health. Some of us were mere skeletons with the skin hanging from our bones.

Worse still, we were all infested with lice. Soap and personal cleanliness were non-existent and in our crammed quarters lice were bound to multiply. Our hair had grown back a little, and there they settled and laid their nits like beads on a string. They settled everywhere, in our clothing as well as on our skin, which we scratched raw in a vain attempt to relieve the intolerable itching. Many girls developed weeping sores on their bodies which refused to heal. The sores attracted more lice. We were like a camp full of lepers, wretched creatures whom everyone avoided like mangy dogs. There was no water to wash with, no soap, no relief. But what was to follow was even worse.

47

The typhus epidemic

Optimistic rumours started circulating at this point about a collapse of German forces on all fronts. The war was hastening to its end and liberation would arrive any week, any day even. We just had to hang on grimly and not succumb to anything: hunger, cold, thirst, malnutrition, lice, fatigue. All had to be kept at bay at any cost by sheer willpower until the end of the war and our liberation.

But we had miscalculated.

Before any liberators arrived, the whole camp was engulfed by a typhus epidemic.

It spread with the speed of an Australian bush fire and in no time killed thousands upon thousands. It was a disease against which we had no defence. In the unequal battle for survival our only weapons were hope and the will to live.

All of us fell ill. Fever scorched our bodies, our heads buzzed, our ears went deaf, we were indescribably thirsty and, worst of all, crippled with diarrhoea.

Yet we still had to go to work. Sickness was not recognised. We deteriorated rapidly. Girls dropped to their knees on the work shifts, fainted on roll-call. Continence became impossible. The disease had struck us unawares, insidiously, like a sly assassin putting a dagger to our throats.

Like lightning it spread to the remotest corner of the

furthest block. There was no escape. Every day saw the death toll rocketing. With all communications destroyed, the camp was cut off from any source of supply. Bread, our only food, ceased to arrive. All we had left was water and air. The Germans themselves put the final nail in our coffin and cut off the water. Every tap ran dry. Water had meant life. To have typhus and not have water meant death.

In our despair we started drinking water from a tub that had been used for dirty underclothing and was unspeakably polluted. However revolting it was, we scrambled for a sip. After a few days the tub was empty. Many litres of its stinking contents had flowed down our throats and through our guts. Though we all knew the danger, we had freely opted for death in preference to the torture of thirst.

The situation was soon calamitous. Some women were too weak to get up from the bunks and go to the latrines, and their excrement ran down on to those below. There was no one to clean the blocks; the German guards no longer appeared. They had left us to our fate.

We were finally transferred to a block where there was no work duty, the penultimate stage before death. Hardly able to stand, some 300 women were crammed together, one lying on top of another on the bare concrete floor. Lydia was separated from me and assigned to another block, despite my entreaties to leave us together.

The next day I somehow found the energy to go and look for her. She was sitting on the floor leaning against the wall next to another young girl she had quickly made friends with. She was so changed, I felt I had never seen her before: pale and thin, seven months pregnant, with sunken eyes and parched lips. There was nothing I could do for her, but I promised to come again the next day.

We were strictly forbidden to leave our own blocks. But I could not abandon Lydia, and I kept my word. I sneaked into her hut the next day. But the place where she had sat the day before by the wall was empty. Lydia wasn't there. Her new friend told me what had happened.

"Lydia had to use the bucket during the night and it fell out. She miscarried. She didn't know what it was. It drowned in the muck anyway. They took her off to the sick-bay." A stinking hole full of corpses.

I went off staggering from block to block to look for her. Finally I traced her. It was already evening. She was lying in a corner on a bare board, half dead. When she saw me her eyes lit up faintly with joy and gratitude. It was her last spark of life. She held my hand and would not leave go, beseeching me not to leave her there alone. But I had to go back to my own block. I came again as early as possible the next day.

Lydia was no longer there. The board she had been lying on was empty.

She was seventeen.

48

Condemned to death

It was April now. Conditions grew worse. Hundreds of women were dying each day. Everyone dreamed of some magic rescue, but none came from any quarter. Death was all we had to wait for.

One night Blanka succumbed. She, who seemed the toughest of us all, decided she could go on no longer, and had no desire to. Anyone who gave up the struggle was dead in a few hours. As if on demand, death would come and mercifully end all the suffering.

Five days later Anita died. She had not willed it; indeed, she had fought against it. Until her last breath she had been buoyed up by the thought of that happy reunion with Pavel when they would go to the cake shop together. But exhaustion and dehydration overcame her stamina. She fell into a delirium and raved, until her lips went blue and she died. The two women on either side of her dragged her by the arms and threw her on the great pile of corpses in front of the hut.

I was the only one of the group left now. It was the first time it had occurred to me that I might die here like the others. I had never conceived of this thought – until now. I was just a mass of bones with the skin hanging in folds like crumpled paper. Eyes and teeth were all that was left of my face. My muscles had disappeared and, because of the diarrhoea, my intestines hung out of me like those of a sick animal. I could no longer stand or walk, but lay inertly on the bare floor amid the dust, dirt and excrement. There were corpses, many already decomposing, in the room among the living. We all looked so similar now that it was hard to tell who was dead and who was still breathing. Those who were alive lay with staring eyes, watching and waiting for the Reaper to come around with his scythe.

There was no one to bury the dead. Those few inmates who could still stand would try and drag the corpses out onto the piles that rose steadily among the birches – those trees that had so delighted me when we arrived. Higgledy-piggledy mountains of human refuse. There were other bodies just lying in the mud wherever death had chanced upon them.

The whole camp was turning into an open cemetery.

Hopes of survival were fast evaporating. It was clear that the Germans were going to let us die here down to the last prisoner. The Reaper worked overtime, the death toll rose mercilessly, and nothing seemed likely to halt it.

Death is such a simple matter. Fancy funerals with wreaths, music and gravestones? No such thing here. A little hole in the ground would suffice, with a handful of soil strewn over the spot where the bones could mingle with the dust of the earth.

Unless help came quickly, it seemed the whole camp would be wiped out. Help from outside. That was the miracle the breathing ones were waiting for, the very last ember of hope still glimmering in our hearts.

49

The British

Finally, one morning, I think it was 15 April 1945, when I was lying on the ground in my last throes among the dead and the living, I heard a high-pitched cry, "They're here! They're here!"

"Who are?"

"The British, of course!"

"Oh, hmm," echoed the faint answer, no longer with any interest. The moment we had been yearning for throughout the long war years, that shone in the distance for us like a lighthouse showing us the way, the topic of every conversation, the subject of endless fantasies, the moment not only we but the whole world had waited for, found us as apathetic as if it hardly concerned us. We were beyond noticing the world around us, for all the life left in us. We felt no sadness. We had no tears. No emotion stirred us. Just that final drop of energy that kept us breathing. That was all.

The arrival of the British army had no visible effect in our block, the remotest in the camp. We were all in need of immediate aid and attention, and this was impossible.

I cannot say what impression Belsen made on outsiders unprepared for what they found here. Presumably they first had to establish priorities – like picking up the corpses that lay around, 13,000 of them. Heavy bulldozers started driving through the camp, pushing the bodies into enormous, freshly dug, communal graves.

To speed things up the former German camp guards, now prisoners of the British army, had to load the remaining ones onto open trucks and take them to the pits. Arms and legs hung over the sides of the trucks. To prevent the corpses from sliding off during the ride, the guards sat on them as one might sit on sheaves of hay in a cart bringing the harvest home. What a happy occasion that used to be! But here in Belsen it was the devils themselves who were now bringing their own harvest in.

Our liberators had certainly brought food supplies with them, but nothing reached our block at the far end. Perhaps those in charge of other blocks along the line kept everything for themselves. We now heard that the sick were being evacuated from the camp to the nearest German military point, Bergen, where some barracks were being used as a hospital for them. They were doing it systematically, block by block. But our block was the furthest away. I began to doubt if they would ever get to us in time.

Several days had now elapsed since the British came. But we were not counting in days any more, only in hours. Like the others around me, I lay motionless on the floor in a delirium, mumbling pleas for water, water …

Hallucinations from a long-forgotten way of life appeared before me. My father sending me to the inn for beer … sitting on the steps and sipping the cold, white froth from the mug … my mother ordering a glass of red fruit drink with a straw for me in an outdoor restaurant, all cold and bubbly … coming to some old ruins on a school outing, where a stall sold lemonade and lemon and raspberry soda in glass bottles, with a rubber washer hidden under the stopper … sitting on the grass beside the path, drinking from the bottle … doing harvest work, raking the hay … sitting in the field at noon … the farmer's wife comes along with a great jar of cold, sour milk … I hold it in my hands and drink, drink, drink …

I sensed now that my end was coming. Everyone has his limits. Even the strongest will must succumb.

50

One last effort

But a strange thing happened that evening.

In the wall of the block where I lay was a long, narrow crack through which a beam of electric light shone from outside. I gazed at it, mesmerised.

Somehow the light turned into a voice that spoke clearly to me:

"You can go no further. This is the end for you."

I listened to it, but then, from somewhere inside me, came another voice as if in answer. An eerie voice that might have been the final instruction of my inner survival kit, "No!" it said. "Not yet!"

Suddenly I felt a surge of supernatural strength that forced me onto my feet and commanded, "Get out! Get away from here! Quick, this is your last chance!"

Where had this burst of strength come from? This superhuman power I never knew existed? How did I summon up this mysterious force to help achieve the impossible? Whence did it emanate? Does everyone possess it when life is in mortal danger? Or only some of us? Was it the Holy Spirit that religion speaks of? Or God himself?

I'll never know how, but I pulled myself together, climbed over all the bodies strewn on the floor, alive and dead, and stumbled out from the block.

Crawling on my knees over the wet yellow clay, I pushed on and on in no particular direction, away at all costs from the block where I had stared death in the face.

As I crawled I slurped up water from the puddles like a thirsty dog.

On and on I crept around the corpses scattered on the ground, until suddenly my strength gave out. I gasped for breath as my last thought ran through my head, "This is the end. So I didn't win, after all." Then I fainted.

Who knows how long I lay there in the mud, but after a while I came to.

I felt rather puzzled. That last voice that had come to me from the unknown, had it spoken true when it said, "Not yet"?

I stayed on the ground for a moment. No one noticed me. One more of us, or less. Who cared?

It was dark now. All I could see was a building in front of me, lit up. Squinting towards the light I made out that I was lying in front of a Red Cross post with the symbol on the door. What angel had directed me here?

The right-hand door opened onto a long corridor. I crawled inside.

The left-hand door was shut. Behind it three stretchers were arranged along the wall, one on top of the other. I squatted in the corner between the closed part of the door and the stretchers, thinking, what a pity I don't have the strength to climb up on to the top stretcher and lie down on it. Never mind, I am used to lying on the floor. After a while the lights went out and the door was locked, presumably by the last person on duty leaving.

I felt safe. I had given the Grim Reaper the slip, just when he had been standing over me ready to swing his arm. With that I fell asleep. The sound of a key in the lock woke me up. Someone had walked in and switched on the light.

A British officer in his military uniform and beret was standing in front of me.

My eyes lit up. Not a German guard with a whip this time, but a real Englishman.

My saviour, my friend! Or was he? Perhaps I was wrong.

As soon as he saw me he asked very sternly: "What are you doing here?"

I answered him in my best English, as if it were my mother tongue, "Nothing. I'm just sitting here." Which was true enough.

But he must have had his orders and he reacted in military style, "You can't stay here. You have to go back to your own block and wait your turn to be evacuated. I must ask you to leave right away. We have a lot to do here."

No doubt he was right. But he could not know that my life was hanging on a thread. That I had not even the strength to find my way back to the death block.

Still standing over me, he repeated his order.

"Please leave."

I have always been obedient and anxious not to cause trouble. But something different was at stake this time: my life. I was well aware that going back to my block would be an instant death sentence.

I could not at any cost do as he asked.

I looked him straight in the face and spoke to him in a quiet but determined tone.

"I understand what you say," I said. "You have your instructions and your job is not easy. You have been here a few days and seen what you have seen. The value of human life here is nil. Myself, I just can't take any more. I know with absolute certainty that if I go back to my own block I shall be dead by morning. Please let me stay here in this corner. I assure you I will live and you will have saved at least one human being. But if it is against your instructions,

I will not stand in your way. I would then ask you to shoot me now."

He stood looking at me and said nothing.

Then suddenly his features moved, as if in a film, the military mask dropped and beneath it showed a human face, full of compassion and understanding.

"Very well then," he said, "you stay here. I shall see that no one touches you. I will come for you in the morning."

"Have you any water, please?" I sighed.

"One moment." He disappeared up the long corridor and brought back a jug of clean drinking water.

"Thank you," I gasped.

I took the jug in both hands and emptied it in one draught. This was not water out of a filthy tub, or a muddy yellow puddle, but clean, clear water. The water of life.

He left, and locked the door behind him.

51

My lucky star

I believed his promise and waited. The next morning the corridor was full of people. No one took any notice of me. Finally, he appeared: my saviour, just as he had said. He arrived in a military ambulance, which he backed up to the exit, and opened the back door. There were four stretchers inside, two on each side on top of each other. But what did I see? All of them were occupied. Where was he going to put me?

I need not have worried. He brought in a spare stretcher and propped it against the wall. Then stepping up to me he ripped off the lousy, tattered, green evening dress I had been given six months before in Auschwitz and never taken off, threw it into a corner with an extra kick, and wrapped me swiftly in a white sheet. Lifting me like a feather he strapped me onto the spare stretcher and took me to the ambulance. He then fitted me in crossways between the others. No doubt it was against all the rules to have five stretchers in use.

He got behind the wheel and we drove off. There was a wide gap in the door behind me. I turned around a little, and I could see Belsen retreating into the distance – and into the past. Here I was, my naked life wrapped in a sheet with only my tin ring hanging on a string around my neck, the symbol of my love and hope that helped me to cheat death.

I felt a new surge of energy now. After Belsen, nothing worse could ever happen to me. So I would live on.

———✳———

What had been in my mind that time, five years earlier, when I first heard Fred Astaire singing *You are my lucky star*? Why had I felt such an intense desire to learn English, almost knowing I would need it one day?

Was it Fred Astaire who showed me the way? It was certainly his song that had brought me this far. My fate was almost sealed when, in what seemed the final moment of my life, I managed to communicate in English with my English saviour. May God bless the country that sent him.

When I was on the very brink, already slipping down into the dark depths forever, this Englishman suddenly appeared, stretched out his helping hand over the abyss, and pulled me back into life.

So, that was him, then: my lucky star.

Some British officer whose name I do not even know.

My Unknown Warrior.

I cannot even thank him in person.

And he will never know how grateful I shall always be for the rest of my days for his act of humanity. He saved my life.

52

The war ends

We arrived in Bergen, a garrison town occupied by the British. They took us out on our stretchers, laid us down on long stone tables and scrubbed us with brushes and carbolic soap to get rid of the lice that were still crawling over us. Finally they dusted us with DDT powder and billeted us four at a time in little rooms strewn with straw. There we lay on the floor, one in each corner.

Although we were safe at last, the typhus continued to work its way remorselessly through our bodies. We were strangers; the one next to me was a Hungarian, I think, and probably the other two as well. We had no contact; each of us was living in her own world, fighting for her own life. One of them lost the battle and died during the night.

Slowly they began to feed us. The days passed and our consciousness moved as if through a misty landscape. Most of the time we just slept.

Then one day the word got around that the war had ended. Ended? I could not grasp what it meant. It was a day like any other and during the night both of my two remaining roommates died in the straw.

Who, of all my friends, were still alive? There could not be many of them. Nana Krásová, Anita Kohnová, Blanka Krausová, my sister Lydia – all had perished, one after the other. Of the thousand girls who stood before the gas chamber in Auschwitz and were sent to Kurzbach, who stumbled along the marches and were crushed in the trains, only seventeen survived – and I was one of them.

"Zdenka, you will be the only one of us to survive," Nana had prophesied that night in Kurzbach. The fact gives me no joy. What am I doing here, I asked, when all those around me have gone? And all for no reason. What was the point of it all? Whose interest was served? The world will go on, but will it be any better than before? Human nature will be as it always was. No one will learn any lesson from history.

———✦———

Now that I alone remained they moved me to a larger room with an iron military bedstead. A real luxury. To have a whole bed to oneself! But I still couldn't get up. I weighed 77 pounds and when they made my bed they had to lay me on the ground, as my legs wouldn't support me. It was only now that I really became aware of my state of health, which I had never thought about when I was struggling to survive. But I knew I was in good hands. The British looked after us as best they could. I started mentally preparing for my homecoming.

Who would turn up first? Father? Mother? Jirka? Not Lydia now. Or would I be first, perhaps? And then Arno. Where might he now be? What would he have gone through and what would he look like? We hadn't seen each other for three years. I felt sure he would come back and everything would be just as we had promised one another. He would be pleased that I had worn his ring around me all that time as a lucky charm, and that it had protected me and given me strength along the way.

As I lay on my iron bed, visions passed through my mind of my homecoming and of our reunion, in all possible variations. Around this time the military authorities at Bergen started to register our details. Each of us was given an identity card with name and number. We even heard they were drawing up lists of people fit enough to be repatriated to their original countries. I could hardly wait for my turn to come.

Simultaneously, however, another project got going, organised by the International Red Cross on the initiative of the Swedish government, to send several thousand seriously ill camp survivors to Sweden for treatment. I had never thought about Sweden. The proposed rescue plan had nothing to do with me; I was sure I would be sent to my own country, and could only hope it would happen soon. I started to feel impatient. The war was over, we weren't threatened from any direction, Belsen was behind me. So let's get home!

In quite a short time the first groups of people were indeed leaving Bergen for their home countries. I longed and longed for my turn to come. But fate decided otherwise.

A member of the British administration came to tell me my name was on a list of patients due to go to Sweden. My disappointment couldn't have been greater. I begged them with tears in my eyes not to send me there. I wanted to go home, not to Sweden where I had no connections and didn't know the language. I must return home! Please! But it was no use. They assured me that I would recuperate and regain my health and strength in Sweden and could then return to my own country whenever I liked.

My bed neighbour now was Erna Luxová from Plzen, who had been through Belsen as well. She was not on the Swedish list but would have liked to be. She sat up on my bed and uttered these memorable words, "Don't be stupid, Zdenka. Go to Sweden, they have real bacon there!"

We were still pretty hungry. We were being fed only a light diet, very sparingly, on account of our deteriorated physical condition. So the idea of bacon became at that moment quite irresistible. Well, I thought, since I'm on the list anyway, I could go there for a bit, get better quickly and return home a fit person? The bacon bait did it.

A harmless little decision on the spur of the moment. Little did I know it would determine the rest of my life. That yen for bacon was to put me on an entirely new track, introduce me to an unexpected future, and open up the world for me.

53

Sweden

All of us on the Sweden list were soon sent from Bergen to the port of Lübeck, where we were put on a large ship already fitted with hospital beds. On 1 July 1945, we sailed past the island of Kalmar and arrived at the town of Norrköping on the eastern coast. We were brought down the gangway on stretchers. I was so curious to see where I was that I twisted around and fell off onto the ground. Such was my first contact with Swedish soil.

They took us to a large modern hospital where we were accommodated four to a room. Each of us had a bed waiting with clean white linen, a fresh-smelling pillow and our own soft, warm blanket. It was something we had only dreamed of all those years. We felt we had come from hell straight into heaven.

We were met by a small reception committee from the emergency service and registered by name and nationality. One of the officials was a Czech, woman living in Sweden, Dr Helena Hájková. She welcomed me like a long-lost relative; we soon became very close and she later helped me a great deal.

We were given excellent treatment and first-class food. For the first time in years I held a cake of scented soap in my hand. In Belsen, after all, we didn't even have water, let alone soap – that was just something to be remembered from a previous existence. And now each of us had a toothbrush, toothpaste, and a comb, things we had not set eyes on since leaving Terezín.

Everyone we met was kind and full of compassion, even though they could hardly conceive what conditions we had come from and what we had endured.

Slowly our physical condition improved and we began to approach normality. We were allowed to walk along the corridors and even take our first tentative steps outside the building in the street. Here we didn't have to wear the Star of David. No one threatened us with arrest. On the contrary, people smiled at us. Our hair grew back and we could recognise ourselves again. The streets were lively, full of traffic, shops and activity. It took us a while to get used to moving among normal people who had never been prisoners. Our spirits rose as our health improved and we looked forward to going home.

Then everything changed.

Official rosters of concentration camp survivors began to appear. Dr Hájková had access to them and brought them to show me. I leafed through them feverishly in the hope that the next day, or the day after, I would spot the names of Arno or my family. They never appeared. Not one of their names was in the lists of the living. Not even in the last one before publication ceased. How was I to cope with this sudden moment of truth, for which I was so unprepared? How was I to accept that every one of those closest to me had perished? Not one would come back any more, not one would I ever see again.

Statistics started appearing about the fate of individual transports to the extermination camps. These established beyond doubt that everyone who was sent "to the left" on arrival at Auschwitz went straight to the gas chambers.

That accounted for Mother. Just as my old acquaintance there had briefly informed me, "she had gone up the chimney." And I thought he was mentally deranged!

I also found out that Arno's "penal transport", in revenge for the assassination of Heydrich, had been sent to Poland in June 1942, where, at a place called Trawniky, everyone was killed on arrival. Arno had had no chance.

The tin ring he had slipped on my finger before he left was all that remained of him.

One day I also learned from a friend of my brother Jirka what had become of him. After his arrival in Auschwitz in the autumn of 1944 he was sent on a transport to Gliwice to build a rocket munitions factory. When the Russian front moved closer in January 1945, he made a bid for freedom, but two SS men caught him escaping and shot him.

About my father, I had not yet been able to establish anything.

———✦———

So no one had survived. No one had returned. Our family had vanished. Even our home, I learned, was already occupied by strangers. It finally dawned on me that I was left completely alone in the world.

Alone in a foreign country, ill, without friends, without any means. All I possessed of my own were Arno's ring and the swastika-engraved knife I had found in the mud at Belsen – my total worldly wealth.

I was engulfed in a wave of despair. For four years I had struggled to survive at all costs. I had never given in. Now, safe and free at last, I had no desire to live, nothing and no one to live for. I wished I had stayed in Belsen with the others – my sister Lydia, Anita, Blanka.

What was I doing here? What good could I be?

Why should I be the only one left? I sank into a deep depression, wondering how one could start a new life from scratch. Begin again from nothing, from exactly zero. The only clothes I had were those I was wearing, donated by the hospital. How could I pull myself together? Where could I start?

I found myself a girl friend, Vera. It's easier to "pull together" as a pair. She had been a dancer in Prague, gone through Belsen, and was now also alone with no idea where to turn. We teamed up and felt better immediately. We decided to stay in Sweden for a bit and then think what to do next. We had nowhere to go back to at the moment, and no one was expecting us. Other people were already living in our old homes. Before we could start rebuilding our life, brick by brick, we had to face the task of laying a new foundation, inch by inch.

54

On the production line

The Swedish government offered anybody who wanted to stay there, and had nowhere else to go, the right of residence with social benefits. To give us the chance of earning our own living we would be offered jobs in industry. Vera and I were given places in a biscuit factory at Kungälv in southern Sweden.

We found a room and board with a family called Johanson. They were very kind people and took good care of us. But they lived outside the town, about an hour's walk from the factory. Work started at 7.30 a.m.

We found ourselves on a production line along with twenty older, experienced packers. The job seemed simple to us at first. A paper box, marked out, had to be folded in two, nine biscuits put inside, undamaged, and the packet passed further along the moving belt. The production norm was 140 packets filled per person per hour. For packers who had spent half a lifetime on the job, it was child's play. But we kept breaking biscuits, couldn't fold the paper fast enough and were generally lagging behind. We only managed about 70 packets an hour, which held up production considerably.

The old hands, who had seen us as intruders from the start, spotted it immediately and complained to the foreman. One day he came to tell us we would have to be shifted from the production line to lighter work with lower pay. Though the job and the whole way of life was hardly our ideal and didn't offer any prospects for the future, we felt rather like Chaplin in *Modern Times*. We were determined to achieve the 140-packets-per-hour target. If the others could do it, so could we.

"You know what?" I said to Vera. "You're a trained seamstress and good with your hands, and I've got a pianist's fingers, so let's take a few boxes home with us and see if we can fold them faster. I bet you we can do it. Somehow we must manage to stay on the production line."

I talked to the foreman in some Babel of languages and begged him to let us carry on for one more week. The strategy worked. Instead of going to bed we tried and tried to find a new way to fold the paper until we succeeded. We surprised ourselves at how quickly it went. In exactly a week we were able to turn out not just 140 packets an hour, but 165! No one had ever reached that figure. The old hands who had felt no particular love for us before, positively hated us now! But the foreman was pleased and let us stay in the job.

However, it was a drab, unvarying life. On top of the monotonous work and the long walks back and forth to the factory, there was nothing for us when we got to the house – just fatigue, and sleep. We felt time stretching out cheerlessly before us into an empty future, not a spark of hope on the horizon that anything might change. A spell of deep depression descended on us at the thought of spending the rest of our lives packing biscuits.

"We'll never get out of here!" I wept on Vera's shoulder. She tried to cheer me up, "Don't you worry. You'll see us both ending up in places where we belong." But she couldn't really figure out how.

However, unexpected things often happen. One day there was a telegram for me from Dr Hájková:

CZECH EMBASSY IN STOCKHOLM LOOKING FOR CZECH SECRETARY. MEET YOU AT 16.15 HRS THURSDAY, STOCKHOLM MAIN STATION.

We hadn't counted on this, a career opportunity falling into my lap. But, as a good pal, I felt I had to reject it. "I can't take a job in Stockholm and leave you alone in this ghastly factory! We must stick together and I'll forget the Thursday date. I'm not going!"

"You must be crazy!" Vera swore back at me. "Of course you'll go! Can't you see that this is our only chance of escaping from here? You're sure to get the position and move to Stockholm. I'll follow you as soon as I can and we'll be together again – but there and not here."

I had to admit she was right. So off I went and boarded the train to Stockholm, dressed as best as I could. I was scared stiff. Supposing Dr Hájková wasn't on the platform? Where would I go next, not knowing a soul? How would this all end up?

In fact, Dr Hájková was there and greeted me with enthusiasm. We took a taxi straight to the embassy. The new ambassador, Dr Eduard Táborský, former secretary to President Beneš, was expecting us in his office.

After a short formal introduction he said, "I see you've had a Czech education, and we need a Czech secretary here right away. But do you know enough Swedish to work the switchboard and answer the phone?" Now I became aware that my future depended on my answer to this question. I also knew that any switchboard was beyond my technical prowess, in any language, and worse still, that all I could say in Swedish was "yes", "no" and "tack så mycket" – thanks.

Wild ideas and sheer panic gripped me. Then the words of advice from my father flashed through my mind: "Never say there's anything you can't do. Remember, if an elephant can learn to walk on bottles in a circus, there's nothing *you* can't master."

The ambassador sat waiting for my answer.

I looked him straight in the face and said, "Yes, I do."

"Very well. You can start on Monday."

———✳———

I returned to Kungälv and gave in my notice. To my surprise I was handed a testimonial from the factory as the best biscuit packer they'd ever had. I put my scraps of clothing in my case, bade Vera a temporary farewell, and took the train to Stockholm. There I found a room right away in the Birgerjarlsgatan, only a few minutes' walk from our embassy at No. 15 Nybrokajen.

Now my problems really began. My first week on the switchboard was like a nightmare. The language problem made it even worse. I couldn't catch a word of what people said over the telephone. I soon learned to repeat their phrases in parrot-fashion without knowing what I was saying. But I knew this was a problem I had to conquer at all costs, and mighty quickly.

I bought a dictionary and piles of newspapers, sat over them night after night and tried to make sense of them. Study, study, listen, listen, talk, talk. Gradually I sensed that I was digging my way out of this dark tunnel of non-communication into the daylight, where I began to understand what people were saying and even to answer them in Swedish.

The office work, among a small group of Czech women, was varied and interesting. We were often invited to take part in official events in honour of prominent people and VIP guests. Soon there were invitations to good restaurants, and new clothes; the world began to open up. The biscuit production line vanished into the past.

Vera soon came to join me and our life started to work out as she had foreseen. She quickly found a job as a seamstress, though she really wasn't one by profession, in one of the big stores. We were starting to enjoy life together now. We never quite got used to the long, dark Nordic winters, though, or the short summer months whose long days flowed into one another without any proper night in between. Still, we gradually returned to normal life.

One day I had a surprise letter from someone I had never heard of, a Dr J. Lederer of Prague. He had found my name on a list of extermination camp survivors, and wrote that he had been with my father in Auschwitz for several months. They had left in January 1945, when the camp was wound up, and he had been on a death march with my father when he died two weeks later.

Dr Lederer described how courageous Father had been, encouraging people around him, and said he had often talked about me. It was his dearest wish that I should survive. He was convinced I would. Dr Lederer invited me to Prague to tell me everything about my father, as they had been together until the end. He said how pleased he would be to meet me.

I knew that I should go to Prague to meet Dr Lederer as soon as possible. Chance played into my hands; one of our embassy staff was driving back to Prague for Christmas and offered me a lift. We drove right through Germany. The German cities had been levelled and, in 1946, were still in ruins. Scorched brick, twisted wire, broken stairways and piles of rubble were all that remained of people's homes.

Divine retribution?

Prague rose before us in all its beauty: pristine, majestic, untouched by the fury of war. First thing the next day I set out to achieve the only purpose of my trip and meet this Dr Lederer face-to-face. He lived in a large apartment house on Dlouhá Trída in central Prague. The lift was broken. I walked up to the third floor.

There was his front door, in carved brown wood. On the left was a white doorbell with a copper plate above it, DR J. LEDERER.

My finger was poised. All I had to do was push the bell. Suddenly I decided I didn't want to know anything or hear anything more about my father. No details about his sufferings, or how or where he had died. I could still see him standing in the doorway, in full command of himself as the Gestapo led him off, raising his hat to us and saying, "Just keep calm. Remember, calmness is strength."

That was how I wanted to remember him.

My hand dropped from the doorbell. I slowly walked downstairs and out on to the street. I never met Dr J. Lederer. With this decision I closed the final chapter of our family album and put it deep down into the safe box of my memory.

Two days later I returned to Sweden. Much as I longed for my native town in Bohemia, I didn't return to my home again until fifty years later.

Many people wonder what happened after Sweden. Well, I went to Australia where I married and had a daughter. I now have two granddaughters and a great grandson, all living in America. Here is how it happened.

55

Christmas in London

Fate is forever offering me a helping hand. It was winter 1946 in Stockholm. My father's uncle, who I had never heard of, suddenly appeared. Walter Fantl, who was my grandfather's brother, had moved to Vienna as a young man, a city where he had liked living and stayed. After Hitler's Anschluss he didn't want to await further political developments. He married his girlfriend quickly and they both left for England, where they started a new life. They settled in a small flat in London where they lived happily. They had no children.

When they discovered that I was the only one from the whole family who had survived the war, they invited me to London for Christmas. I was touched by their offer. If I accepted, I would make them very happy. I would travel to England by ship... ship? Suddenly it felt as if a door was opening for me into a new life and world. The thought that I would be spending Christmas with a family in London instead of being, sadly, on my own in Sweden made me very happy. London! Large city! World's metropolis! What would it do for me? It would be an unforgettable experience. So many things to see there! And I would not be on my own but with an experienced guide. I was, impatiently, looking forward to my journey, sailing from Gothenburg.

The ship docked at Tilburg and from there I travelled to London by train. Everything I saw from the train was completely different from what I had seen in Sweden. First I noticed small, low chimneys, sometimes in clumps on every roof. In other places there were houses with one storey only, which stood in small gardens. At times it looked like groups of them together, as if they were holding hands; but chimneys, chimneys everywhere. In England, every house has its fireplace and each has its own chimney. Smoke goes out of them and it tells the world the house is cosy. An open fire gives a family warmth and a feeling of togetherness. Although it was just before Christmas, there was no snow and the trees had bare branches. Each house had its own garden which was divided by a low wall from their neighbours and the street. "My house, my castle".

When I disembarked from the train at a big station in the centre of London, there was a terrific welcome, tears and happiness. In their small but cosy flat in Chalk Farm the talk, food and drink went on and on. Uncle Fantl, as I called him, was amusing company, well-informed and loved life.

"I'll show you London today," said my uncle. We drove into the centre. On both sides of the streets there were big, solid buildings from past centuries and the glory of the British Empire. We saw Buckingham Palace – the royal residence; Hyde Park Corner with a victory statue; Park Lane full of opulent hotels; vast Hyde Park with its large lake and the huge round building of the Royal Albert Hall opposite. London, a remarkable and beautiful city, was still carrying the marks left on it by the war. This was 1946, when the city was just waking up to a new life, like a patient who had suffered a serious blow and, by some miracle, survived. Everywhere there were signs of those battles. Walls with damaged surfaces and piles of debris everywhere. Whole areas, such as the south bank of the river, had been bombed and were now deserted. We saw Trafalgar Square with Nelson's Column, Whitehall with Downing Street, the buildings of the Parliament with Big Ben and opposite, Westminster Abbey and St Paul's Cathedral. I also had to try a trip on a red double-decker bus. It seemed that just about every corner housed a Lyon's Corner tea house – coffee was not very popular in England then.

Towards the end of my stay, there was going to be a big farewell dinner and friends of Uncle Fantl and his wife were invited. Mr and Mrs Barnes were lovely company. "How do you like living in Sweden?" was their question.

"Like it or not, I live there and do not have any other choice. I am grateful to Sweden for accepting me and for making sure I had another start in life. I shall do my best to be of use. At the moment I have a good and an interesting job at the Czechoslovak Embassy which I like very much. When the post-war situation in Czechoslovakia gets sorted out I would like to return to my native country."

"Would you consider going to Australia and set-tling there?" asked Mr Barnes. "My brother lives there, in Melbourne. He is doing really well. He could send you a Landing Permit which is the only document necessary for immigration. The Australian government are trying to get more European immigrants for their country."

"To Australia? Where is it ? It is somewhere at the end of the world?" His suggestion amused me and, smiling I added, "It is very kind of you to suggest that and that your brother would organise the Landing Permit, but what would I do there? I am not a gold-digger or a sailor, and strange, distant countries do not interest me. I'll stay where I am and later return to my own country. Thank you very much for your offer but Australia is not for me."

At the time I felt that Australia, thousands of miles away from the rest of the world was distant from my roots, ambitions and plans. The evening continued in a pleasant atmosphere and we parted friends. I forgot Australia and the following day I returned to Sweden.

56

Working at the Czech Embassy

On my return from England I went back to my job at the Embassy, where I felt I knew my position and work. My Swedish was much better now. Among my Czech colleagues I felt as though I was on a small Czech island in foreign waters. The Ambassador, Eduard Taborsky, formerly the secretary to President Benes, led the office and staff with his firm and capable hands. His professional diplomatic style, experience and abilities were all creating a very good name for Czechoslovakia in Sweden. In my job I had a variety of duties – a bit of a Girl Friday. I handled the Embassy switchboard, and translated pertinent newspaper articles concerning Czechoslovakia, which were then sent in a diplomatic bag to the Foreign Office in Prague. For official Czech visitors, I organised whatever they needed and whatever was necessary. Often I would take them gift shopping before their return to Prague.

The Ambassador also asked me to arrange more interesting things such as meetings with various well-known personalities who turned up in Stockholm. One such visitor was the German writer Thomas Mann; another the legendary Swedish writer Axel Munthe, whom the Ambassador admired. When it came to Embassy entertainment which took place at the Residence, I had to order food for a given number of people.

At one stage I had special work lined up which turned into two months of entertaining in Stockholm. Together with the cultural section of the Embassy I had to organise a visit from several members of the Czech PEN Club in Prague and two notable sculptors – Jan Kodet and Vincenc Vingler. Both sculptors would remain in Stockholm for several weeks and would exhibit their work in a famous gallery in the capital.

When the Delegation arrived, the PEN personnel were led by Frantisek Langer, a writer in whose play *Camel Through an Eye of a Needle* I acted in Terezin during the war. When I told him about it, he expressed interest in our theatrical activities and was visibly pleased the play was a success there.

At the exhibition, Jan Kodet had, among his works, many nudes in various shapes and positions. Vingler was interested in and sculpted many different animals, their moods and their importance in human life. His most famous sculpture was a sitting monkey that looked like a human female beggar. Maurice Chevalier, who was then performing in Stockholm, came to the opening. Not only was he impressed by both artists, but he bought one of Kodet's best works. The Swedish King Gustav also came to see the exhibition and was interested in the animal sculptures, particularly that of a small elephant – as if with a smile on his face – which he bought, apparently for good luck. The owner of the biggest Swedish ceramics company also came to visit the exhibition. He took a good look at all the exhibits and, without hesitation, he pointed at the monkey, which he bought immediately. He also acquired the reproduction rights. Vingler's monkey has appeared in many Swedish houses.

During my time at the embassy, a communist putsch took place in Czechoslovakia. All members of the diplomatic staff decided not to return to Prague. I was kept in my job by their replacements. As I was a locally employed person, the situation in my home country looked dangerous for people who had contacts with the "west" and I was warned not to return to Czechoslovakia.

I remembered the "Landing Permit" for Australia which had been sent to me by my Uncle Fantl's friend, Mr Barnes, though I had refused it at the time. I decided to take it up and leave. A Dr Hajkova, who had helped me many times before, agreed with my move and was extremely helpful in organising the trip.

57

Journey to Australia

When the day came to leave Stockholm, I travelled to Paris where I spent a few days with a friend enjoying the city. Then, goodbye, and on to Genoa, where a ship would take me to Australia.

In Genoa we could see, swaying gently, the ship which was to take us to Australia. Its name was the *Cyrenia*, sailing under a Panamanian flag with a Greek and Italian crew. It seemed to me, comparatively speaking, rather small for such a long and demanding journey carrying around a thousand passengers.

Waiting to register, I heard someone ordering their children in Czech, "Zuzanka don't run anywhere, hold Mummy's hand or else you could get lost and we would sail without you. Thomas, look after her!" The speaker was Karel Rehn from Prague, with his wife and two children – one of many people who left a very good position at home and chose to emigrate over growing political oppression. He was an extremely bright man who proved himself a merry companion and a brilliant organiser. His two beautiful children, two and five years old, were inquisitive and lively.

Now I started to hear a lot of Czech around me. There were groups of young men who had run away by crossing the border illegally over the mountains and for whom emigration was an adventure. There were also a number of other Czechs, Poles and Hungarians who had come from German Displaced Persons camps. Now we were all on our way to Australia. The mood among the passengers was friendly and optimistic, though no-one really knew where we were going, what was awaiting us there or how we would adjust to a new life in so distant and, to us, completely unknown a country. But around me Czech was spoken! I felt as if I had found a piece of (my) home ground under my feet. I was among my own people. The Rehn's took me in as another member of their family and our friendship continued and grew throughout their lives.

On board the ship we were allocated our cabins. Mine was two levels below the main deck. There were two sets of bunk beds and a small window. I quickly took one of the top bunks so that I would have "control", following my well tested (concentration camp) habit. I do not remember any of the other cabin's travellers. My thoughts were elsewhere and all my attention was concentrated on the instructions about what to do if the ship started sinking.

At that moment, I did not appreciate that I was leaving Europe, and emigrating to a strange, distant continent; I felt more like I was going on an interesting outing.

We docked in Alexandria. The ship was immediately surrounded by people in small boats selling souvenirs. They shouted, "Buy, buy, it is cheap, little money". But we were more interested in the fact that we were allowed to disembark and go to visit the port. We didn't see much, only many exotic-looking people running around and trying hard to sell us African souvenirs – small cushions covered in zebra skin, figures of monkeys and giraffes cut out of wood, etc.

The ship sailed and we entered the Suez Canal which was much narrower than I imagined. I stood at the railings on deck in order to see Africa. Except there was nothing to see, only a vague image I had from my school years. When, at last, we were on the open sea my travels to distant and exotic lands started to interest me.

On the ship was another Czech migrant, Count Frederick Kinsky, an aristocrat, who was going to New Zealand. He was a very well-educated man, familiar with the world, who always carried a pair of binoculars. As I got to know him, I learned about the life and fate of Czech aristocracy and about his childhood. His father, German, didn't allow him to attend school but instead gave him a Czech tutor – a hunter, forester and a great teacher of nature. From him Frederick learnt all he knew about plants, trees and mostly about birds, which later stood him in good stead in his career as a naturalist.

When we reached Colombo, Count Kinsky suggested we take a taxi trip to town. There were about five of us, with Kinsky as a guide. Around us were lots of different people, giving us curious and suspicious looks. We entered a spacious Buddhist temple where we were met with a strong scent from large white blooms, hanging in bunches on the walls. It did not seem as if they were just a decoration, but, perhaps, they had another, deeper meaning. On another street we entered a Hindu temple, much smaller, where there was quite a different "scent". Instead of flowers there were many small brown monkeys. At a local bazaar we didn't have much time to inspect all the foreign-looking objects. But I noticed a stall selling whole branches of bananas and I couldn't resist the temptation. Having bought one, I put it over my shoulder like a trophy won in a tombola and proudly carried it to our ship. Our Czech group sat on the deck in a circle, sang tramp songs and everyone got a banana from me.

We left Colombo and the Bay of Bengal towards evening. Ahead of us was the longest stretch of the journey, maybe a week, on the Indian Ocean, to Western Australia, with no landings. Around us was just water, water as far as the eye could see – as if nothing else existed in the world. "On our left side somewhere far is Sumatra, next to it Java, and a bit beyond it is Borneo," Count Kinsky pointed out. It all sounded exotic – we could not see anything and I simply could not imagine what the distant lands looked like. In my mind I could see the large map of this part of the world which used to hang on the wall during geography lessons at school. It never occurred to me then that I would find myself there. That made me realise that I was a long way from Europe. Even though I could not see anything ahead of me, this feeling was similar to an unusual dream that felt both real and unreal. It was difficult to catch it and place it somewhere.

The journey was very long. We were in the third week of the journey and the sea was endless. The only thing I knew was that at the end of it I would disembark in Australia which, to me, seemed as distant and unreal as all the different and exotic islands and lands we had seen during our passage.

58

Arriving in Australia

The worst part of the journey was ahead of us. We docked briefly in Western Australia and then faced a horrendous week to Melbourne. The sea was so wild I think everyone on board was seasick.

However, everything comes to an end. Towards the evening of 17th September, 1949, we docked in Melbourne. I stood on deck, looking ahead, wondering what might await me.

Before the beginning of the trip I tried in vain to find some information about the country I was about to depart for but there was nothing except a flyer with three photos: Queensland with parrots, a second with crocodiles and a third with some kangaroos. But now here I was, in Australia.

The people waiting at the docks had hats pressed firmly on their heads and looked at us grudgingly as if to say "Why are you coming here? This is our country – what do you want here? We do not want any outsiders here." Sort of an unkind welcome. And unkind was the weather, too, cold and rainy. In spite of it being September, it was still their winter. I didn't even have a coat, as from the sparse information I had expected a hot country.

At the dock was Mr Barnes, the brother of Mr Barnes, who, in London in 1946, offered to get me the Landing

Permit for Australia. Now this Mr Barnes and his girlfriend were waiting for me. They had a car and took me straight to the house of Mrs Moore, 4 Dickens Street, where I was to live as a boarder.

My landlady was an old lady. She showed me into a small, dark room, with iron bars on the small windows. It wasn't the blue sunny skies and open country I was expecting. Mrs Moore had a sitting room (called lounge in Australia) with colourful covers on the settees and an upright piano. I pressed a key and it started playing a tune! I was terrified. An invisible hand was moving across the keys. Although we spoke to each other in English, we did not understand each other well. But she was friendly and ready to help. Australians are like that.

What did the town look like? My first impression was of mostly small red brick, single storey houses, many with corrugated tin roofs. All the streets seemed to lead to the sea. That was strange and great. I had only been to the seaside once, in Yugoslavia, with my family.

I had no idea what I would do or how to keep myself, although we did get some help from a Jewish organization after we arrived. Before I left Sweden, I did a course at Elizabeth Arden on beauty treatments for makeup and manicures, and got a certificate. One of the conditions of coming to Australia was you had to have some kind of trade. So I was a beautician. Mrs Barnes was my first client and she brought two more women. Each client recommended me to someone else, so soon I had a thriving business with four or five clients a day. The rest of the day I was sitting on the beach and my friends were wondering, how could I afford to sit on the beach? They had to work from nine to five at the Holden car factory where they were employing foreigners. Later, a new hairdressing salon opened up nearby. They wanted a beautician, which was a well-paid job, and hired me. So I started to make some money.

59

The wedding reception

One day one of my clients invited me to her wedding and they sent someone to pick me up. At the reception, sitting at a table, was a remarkable-looking man, whose name I later learned was Charles. I could not resist saying hello and he immediately offered me a chair and brought me some food. We talked. He was interested in listening to what I had been through. It transpired that he used to live in Berlin – not a million miles away from Prague.

My stories of concentration camps didn't move him unduly. His whole family was marked by the war. Already in 1933 Germans begged Jewish citizens to leave Germany. Some emigrated and those who stayed behind paid for it, mostly with their lives, including Charles's mother who was put onto an early transport to Auschwitz. She was a talented painter, a lovely woman and Charles could never come to terms with the fact he had not saved her. He had moved to England with his uncle. But in 1940, Britain rounded up and expelled many Germans, regardless of status, as enemy aliens. Charles ended up on board the *Dunera* headed for Australia. Upon arrival they were put into camps. There he met Walter Heine who opened an import/export business, Heine Bros, after the war, similar to one his family had run in Leipzig. Charles was one of the first employees.

He had attended the wedding as a colleague of the bridegroom who also worked at Heine Bros. Charles was a very elegant man with wavy hair, a narrow face; an aristocratic type. He was 36 then. From his eyes two small suns of goodness and warmth shone. This took place in the summer of 1950, around February.

A few days later, I received a card from him, in English. We spoke English together though I spoke decent German. I didn't react immediately but then called him and we agreed to go on a trip by car to Portsea, a lovely town on the coast known for its surf beach. He wasn't a great sport lover, just a slim, pleasant male. I borrowed a board which is quite difficult to learn how to handle. I fell off and lost the board but fortunately the sea brought me to the surface. Charles was horrified – it could have killed me and so I dropped this sport for good. On the journey back, in the little car with the top down, we were confronted with a rather unpleasant event; horses on the road went a bit wild and one of them almost jumped into the car.

For our next outing, Charles suggested a visit to a cinema, called "theatre". There were many theatres in the town. They showed two films. Before the film, a Wurlitzer organ rose up from beneath the stage with someone playing the national anthem, *God Save the Queen*. Then we saw a newsreel followed by a first film, then a long break for refreshments – Eskimo ice cream – then the feature film. On that occasion with Charles, we saw *The Third Man*, starring Orson Welles. After the theatre, Charles took me to a tea room with lace curtains, tea and cakes, and then drove me home.

Meanwhile, I always had Czech company, with Czech songs and talking about things familiar to us "at home" as well. Charles didn't fit in this group though he was friendly with Czechs who visited us at home.

Charles lived on the first floor of a boarding house on Domain Road, not far from the Yarra river. He had his own room and there was a kitchen and bathroom with a two penny water heater, for common use. At the front of the house there was a balcony with a wrought iron railing from which we could see the neon sign for a tomato sauce factory. That scent irritates me to this day.

60

The proposal

One Sunday when I again visited in the evening, Charles made tea and sandwiches and put on a record. It was Mozart's 40th Symphony with the Vienna Philharmonic. Before he put on the record he summed up the courage somehow to steer the conversation to us and ask me to marry him. It was a bit of surprise for me because I wasn't quite ready and didn't have an answer. But I realized what a wonderful man he was. I would be in very good hands, very well looked after and I thought well, why not? He's from Berlin. I'm from Prague. Berlin is not so far away. We came from similar countries with the same upbringing and so on. He was waiting. It was a while before I answered, and said "Yes". I'll never forget Mozart's 40th Symphony, which was right for the occasion, and I remember him being very happy.

That was sometime in February or March 1950. We decided the wedding would be September 24th. Weddings in those days were very modest affairs. We had a little party at home with few friends, no hotels, no big dinners or dresses. I bought a little suit and straw hat. And I moved into his little room.

Since it was the end of winter, we decided to go skiing for our honeymoon to Mt Kosciusko in New South Wales. But when we arrived at the hotel, they told us we have a rule here that women sleep here and the men sleep somewhere else. And we thought well, not exactly what we expected, but it doesn't matter because we can have our fun before and after.

At that time there was no ski sport at all in Australia, which was not known for snow on the mountains. Skiing was practically unknown in Australia until the Czech immigrants came and set up an alpine village in Thredbo which is now very famous.

When we went out with our skis we had to cross rivers. There were no tracks for skiing at all and we had to climb to the top of the mountain. Nobody could understand why we did it.

When we got back to Melbourne there was already a spring blue sky, the sun was shining, and the trees and flowers were in bloom. It was lovely coming back home. We settled in the little flat in Domain Road and over time took over the whole floor. That's where our life started.

Epilogue
Goodbye forever

The elderly lady who came here today after fifty years' absence was still sitting on the pile of planks and looking at the house she had once lived in. Sunk in her memories, she saw the whole story of her life through her mind's eye. Some huge tidal wave, she felt, had passed through here and swept everything away into the sea of oblivion.

Now it was time to say goodbye to the past and go away.

Finally she stood and walked a few paces towards the building. Picking up four small stones from the ground she laid them not on a grave, according to the old Jewish custom, but on the doorstep, in memory of the dead. Her father, her mother, her brother and her sister.

It had got much colder, she felt. She turned away from the house and walked towards the station to catch the train back to Prague.

A man standing on the platform waiting for the same train looked up at the cold grey sky, and then turned to her and said, "Snow will be coming early this year, I reckon."

Photographs

Zdenka's case pictured at the Auschwitz-Birkenau Museum

Arno's ring

Zdenka and Arno, 1940

Zdenka's mother, 1917

Zdenka's father, 1918

Zdenka's brother, Jiri, Zdenka and her mother in July 1925

Jiri, Zdenka's stepmother, Zdenka and her little sister, Lydia, 1931

Zdenka's grandfather Leopold

Lydia with her dog, Punta

Zdenka, Jiri and her friend Vera

Zdenka's father in Luhacovice, 1937

The infamous SS guard, Irma Grese

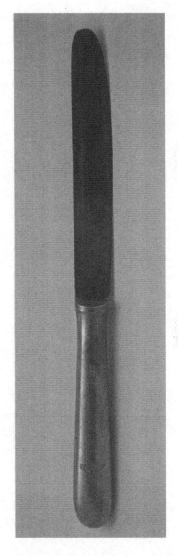

The SS knife used by Irma Grese to attack Zdenka

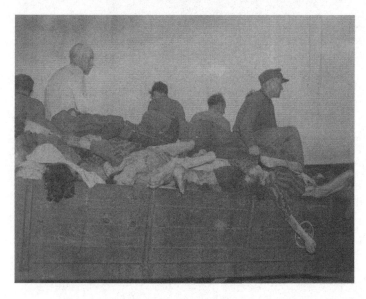

Bergen-Belsen, April 1945

Zdenka as a secretary in the Czech Embassy in Stockholm, 1948

Zdenka Fantlová today

After her liberation from Belsen, Zdenka Fantlová was sent to Sweden for recuperation under the care of the International Red Cross. In 1949, she emigrated to Australia where she married and had a daughter. Since 1969 she has made London her home.

Zdenka's entire family was killed in the Holocaust. She does all that she can to ensure that this dark period in twentieth-century history is never forgotten.

In March 2022, Zdenka celebrated her 100th birthday.

*'Life is wonderful with all its ups and downs.
Every day is a gift'*

Zdenka Fantlová